To Stephen
with love from
Grandmother Heeney.
Christmas 1960

McGILL

THE STORY OF A UNIVERSITY

SPRING CONVOCATION

McGILL

The Story of a University

EDITED BY HUGH MacLENNAN

ILLUSTRATED BY JOHN GILROY

LONDON: GEORGE ALLEN & UNWIN LTD
TORONTO: THOMAS NELSON & SONS (CANADA) LTD

PRINTED IN GREAT BRITAIN
in 11/13 pt. Baskerville type
BY BRADFORD AND DICKENS
LONDON

PREFACE

WERE I a native Montrealer or a graduate of McGill, I don't think it would occur to me to write about this university. Montrealers and McGill men seldom talk publicly about the things they consider important. They never wear their hearts on their sleeves, nor have they troubled to learn the English technique of revealing their hearts through several layers of understatement. Montreal is an intricate city which can be learned only by living in it for years. McGill is an intricate university.

This Montreal habit of reticence is of course a product of the community itself, which is like no other on earth and is in turn the product of a very peculiar history. For two centuries the city has been compelled to live schizophrenically in order to live at all. Two races, or at least two languages, share the living space on Montreal island, and they once were bitter enemies. On many of the grounds which produce murder the two basic linguistic groups of the city are still opposed, yet it is a fact that they do not dislike each other (except sometimes theoretically), and that in the last two centuries they have never seriously offered violence to one another. Tact and compromise, a remarkable talent for sensing the motive of another person, all of this combined with an amused tolerance of public scandal, have made this harmony possible. What Montrealers know best about each other they never say in public. Silence, an experienced and at times a cynical silence, has always been golden here.

This may be why relatively little has been written about McGill University, and why much of what actually has been written has been factual or has been received by insiders with the indifferent shrug of men who understand that what has been written was not intended to reveal truth, but to fill a gap so conspicuous that it had been calling attention to itself. Most Montrealers have a built-in conviction that truth is embarrassing, and in this they are surely realists.

7

Truth often is embarrassing to everybody, and always it is embarrassing to somebody. So is the whole truth about McGill. But the most important thing about McGill is not this, which could be said of any human institution on earth, but the vigour of her growth. And the most unique thing about her is the casual way in which she has taken this growth for granted.

As universities go, McGill is remarkably young; only a century ago she was a tiny, shabby, neglected embryo of a college struggling to keep alive after being born almost moribund. Today she has the air of a veteran, her manners are suave and sophisticated, and to more than one visitor she has the puzzling maturity of a man who has experienced so much that nothing can surprise him, and has muddled through so many confusions that he suspects that any other manner of conducting affairs is sure to fail.

The growth of McGill reminds me of the growth of certain famous families. The first generation is so obscure that nobody notices the family at all, yet a certain direction has been taken, a certain course has been entered, and actions have occurred which we see in retrospect made inevitable at least a few of the future developments. This was McGill during the first forty years after her Founder's death.

In the next generation there appears a family head who is almost a tribal leader. He has the immense inner self-confidence of a limited man of genius. His mind moves tenaciously along a single groove, but because that groove leads forward, and because his energy is enormous, he cannot possibly fail. He expands the family resources, he rules it like a patriarch, he sets it into a mould with many deficiencies and not a few ungainly protruberances. Viewed from one standpoint he is ridiculous, viewed from another he is sublime. He is wrong as only a pig-headed man can be about the value of certain things which the best minds and spirits of all ages have considered priceless, yet he is wrong for reasons natural to his own limited nobility, and about one other thing he is never wrong at all: if a family serves a community to the best of its power, even the most indifferent of communities in the end is sure to support the family. After a life of struggle in which the real gains were immense but the show of them small, the patriarch, now an old and tired man, at last has time to pause and look around him. His work is done, his family is secure, and before it lies a road transcending his imagination. This was McGill under Sir William Dawson.

Then follows a period of expansion in which the family's influence spills widely outside of its own community, without the community being able to realize it. The patriarch had been at one with his community, but his work had transcended it. Now the work—the destiny, if you will–has acquired a life of its own puzzling to its community, an inherent force of its own too great for any one man to control or entirely to direct. Quarrels and misunderstandings appear, there are manipulations for power within the family, and a growing affluence brings its usual train of resentments. This was McGill under Sir William Peterson.

Next comes a generation in which the family, now grown so influential that it takes its influence for granted, more or less marks time while waiting for its brain to catch up with its achievements. This was McGill between the wars when three presidents served her.

After this comes a time when the family, unable to deny the fact that its fortunes are inextricably linked with those of the nation, the nation's problems and needs a reflection of its own problems and needs, seems to be living through a period of frantic adjustment to the sheer pressure of necessity. The family is not only a national institution; its affairs reflect nearly every aspect of the nation's virtues, vices, abilities and limitations. Now at last it is possible to see this family with some sense of proportion. It is possible to recognize that from its birth at the meeting place of the races and rivers, McGill has consistently reflected the enigmatic character of the the nation to which it belongs.

This seems to me the position of McGill under the Principalship of Dr. F. Cyril James. During his incumbency, and he is still a relatively young man, the Canadian population has increased by more than a third and will continue to grow by a kind of geometrical progression. During this same period, the university under Dr. James' charge has more than doubled its enrollment. McGill today is changing faster than ever before. So is the world. And that is hers, and the world's, most immediate and pressing problem.

Hugh MacLennan

September, 1959

CONTENTS

11

ILLUSTRATIONS

13

McGILL

I

McGILL TODAY

BY HUGH MacLENNAN

ALTHOUGH the growth of McGill reflects an international trend since the war, there are few universities where growth has created greater material problems. McGill is located in the heart of the most over-crowded city in Canada, a city on an island like New York, and when you look at the city crowding the campus you wonder how it will be possible for the university to continue to expand in a place where all available land has long ago been occupied. Yet grow she must. Though many McGill men grumble about the rate of her post-war expansion, and some complain that it has altered McGill's character, they never refuse to admit its inevitability. If a university refuses to serve the public, sometimes in ways its lovers believe will upset its harmony, it quickly atrophies and dies.

In her infancy McGill taught only six subjects: Medicine, Classical Literature, Mathematics, Natural Philosophy, Metaphysical and Moral Philosophy. Today she teaches almost everything that can be taught in a modern university, and does so through nine schools and nine faculties, of which the largest, despite those who accuse her of becoming a trade and business school, is still Arts and Science. The other faculties are Agriculture, Dentistry, Engineering, Law, Medicine, Music, Divinity, Graduate Studies and Research. The nine schools are Architecture, Commerce, the French Summer School, the Library School, the School of Household Science, the School for Graduate Nurses, the School of Physical and Occupational Therapy, the School of Social Work, the Institute of Education. A busy extension department teaches a wide variety of courses at night.

Nor is this all. McGill includes within its framework the United and Diocesan College (affiliated with the Faculty of Divinity), the Royal Victoria College, and Macdonald College. Royal Victoria College was separately chartered at the end of the nineteenth century by Lord Strathcona and was the first college for women in Canada. Under a typical nineteenth century pattern of interlocking directorates, the Principal and Governors of McGill are *ex-officio* Principal and Governors of R.V.C., but at the same time one of the duties of the Warden of Royal Victoria College is to represent the interests of all women students in the councils of the University. Macdonald College is situated twenty-five miles away from the main campus at Sainte-Anne-de-Bellevue where stood, in the days of McGill's infancy, the famous little chapel where the *voyageurs* of the Northwest company, in which McGill's founder was a partner, stopped to pray to St. Anne before paddling westward into the wilderness. Macdonald teaches Agriculture, Household Science, home-making courses and contains an institute of education.

There are also eight institutes which might be called collateral members of the McGill family, and their titles indicate the extent to which the interests of this university spill out into the affairs of the modern world. They are: the Institute of International Air and Space Law, the Allan Memorial Institute of Psychiatry, the Arctic Institute of North America, the Institute of Islamic Studies, Staff Development Institutes, the Industrial Relations Institute, the Institute of Parasitology and finally the Montreal Neurological Institute, established and directed by the genius of Dr. Wilder Penfield, o.m. From the beginning, the Neurological has been given strong financial support by one of McGill's most prominent governors.

Before the First World War, McGill could almost have been called the university of English-speaking Montreal, that racial island within the larger racial island of French-Canada. Now she belongs to the world.

During the last thirty-five years the international element in the McGill student body has increased steadily, with the result that today little more than half of the eight-thousand-odd students

come from the Montreal area. Approximately a thousand are from
the other nine Canadian provinces and nearly five hundred are
from the United States. The others come literally from all over the
world – from twenty-one countries of the Commonwealth and from
forty-six nations outside of it. Young men from the sugar islands
and the heart of Africa, from the Mediterranean, from South and
Central America and the Far East come to this northern university
in a land which must seem exceedingly strange and cold to them,
and here they mingle with our own young people with the –
to us – familiar Scottish, English, Irish, Welsh, French and Jewish
names.

For a Canadian university this development is surely remarkable, and the reasons for it are varied. One cause may be the increasingly large role played by Canadian statesmen in international
affairs since the last war. Another may be Canada's senior, and on
the whole popular, status within the Commonwealth. Another
may be a belief that McGill's atmosphere is congenial to strangers,
that if a foreign student dreads the exclusiveness of a tight Anglo-
Saxon community, he can at least take refuge in a bi-lingual city
well known for its tolerance. But the chief cause is certainly McGill's
reputation, especially in science, medicine and engineering. This
reputation was established over many years by McGill graduates
who emigrated to various parts of the world, and above all it rests
on the work of the great teachers and discoverers of knowledge who
founded their fame here and were called, some of them, to other
institutions to which they took some elements of McGill's tradition.

Nothing, it seems to me as a partial outsider, is more typical of
McGill than her attitude toward these great men who were associated with her. She takes hardly any credit for them. The average
McGill man assumes that if they were geniuses, they would have
been geniuses whether they saw McGill or not. He feels it would
be an impertinence to boast about them, and this may be why he
has done so little to commemorate their names on the campus.
Strolling through the campus or wandering about the halls, you
might well wonder if McGill had anyone to be proud of.

A sizable photograph of Sir William Dawson, the formidable
principal who built McGill into a great university in the nineteenth century, hangs in a dark corner of the Arts Building. But I
doubt if one McGill man in a dozen realizes that Dawson, in

The Campus in Winter

addition to being an administrator and a builder, was also a remarkable scientist, much less that his certificate to the Royal Society of London was signed by some of the most eminent men of science of his day, including Darwin and Huxley. I had been around the university for at least six years before I discovered, quite by chance, a minuscule bronze plaque commemorating the epoch-making work of Rutherford during the ten years when he was Macdonald Professor of Physics. In the Physics Building, it is true, Rutherford's old equipment is preserved, but not as a memorial; it is still of interest and value to scientists. Only in 1959 were plaques unveiled in the Chemistry Building to Robert Fulford Ruttan and to Frederick Soddy. Leacock's monument is supposed to be his books. On rare occasions when McGill appears to go all out to honour a man who has been precious to her, the result is likely to be something practical. Sir William Osler is commemorated by a splendid medical library, but it was once his own property: the University merely created a special place for it. Sir Arthur Currie is remembered by an armoury and a gymnasium, but significantly the money for the armoury had previously been donated by Lady Strathcona.

To one like myself, who came to McGill somewhat late in life, this apparent indifference to the outward marks of respect to the great dead seems very healthy. 'The imprint of the personality remains, and what else matters?' So said a McGill man. 'If we built statues to men like Osler and Rutherford,' said another, 'all we would be doing would be to cash in on the credit they won themselves.' A similar attitude prevails towards the most distinguished McGill men now alive and working. At the moment of writing a total of twenty Canadians are members of the Royal Society of London, and of these five are now McGill staff men and three others earned their F.R.S. at the University. Only a few McGill men seem aware of these facts.

Now for the students.

As a body, the students of McGill are not as cohesive as the undergraduates of Oxford or of most Ivy League universities in the United States, and for two reasons. McGill is co-educational and a city university. Almost half the student body lives at home with their parents. The rest are scattered through three university residences, through fraternity houses located on streets near the campus, through lodgings approved by university authorities. Most women students from outside live in Royal Victoria College. From the United States alone, applications for entrance to R.V.C. are so numerous that if all were accepted there would hardly be house room for any Canadians.

Obviously the outside activities and pleasures of students in an urban university depend more upon themselves as individuals than do those of undergraduates in an Ivy League college. The McGill undergraduate is almost on his own. His life is little supervised, and he quickly learns that his university career is not an extension of his career at school. His most serious lack is a sufficient number of playing fields, for land is not available in downtown Montreal. Molson Stadium is a large ampitheatre for football and track, but it contains only one track and only one field and there are more than five thousand male students. There is a rink; there is a gymnasium; there are squash and tennis courts. But if a man is not in a team, sport is not likely to play a large role in his university life unless he contrives to go ski-ing on winter weekends. Before the war, McGill football and hockey teams were famous. They are famous no longer because post-war Canada is turning into a nation of spectators, and Montrealers prefer to watch professional athletes.

These post-war students, the seniors at any rate, show sharper differences of ability than was apparent in universities thirty years ago. The average level of industry seems lower than it used to be. On the other hand the best students, possibly because they are not emotionally inhibited, seem superior to the best in my day. The McGill student body – no doubt of this whatever – is the most sophisticated in Canada. This they proved to the whole nation in 1957 when their *Red and White Review* produced a musical comedy called *My Fur Lady*, which was so competent professionally that it played to packed houses in the commercial theatres of our leading cities. It was a delicious satire on Canadian life, and the closest thing to Aristophanes ever seen on the Canadian stage.

When I think of a university I am inclined to ask, not, ' Where is its knowledge?' but 'Where is its beauty?' And in seeking to answer that question, I sympathize with the traditional McGill men who take it for granted that it is impossible to make other people see their university as they see it themselves.

If McGill were a woman, Rembrandt might have wanted to

paint her; Raphael never. The loveliness of Oxford and Cambridge is palpable and romantic, and has so impressed its image on mankind that North American campuses are littered with copies of Magdalen Tower, Trinity Gateway and the Great Hall of the House. In a North American environment these pious imitations have seemed to more than one European as appropriate as a lock of Keats' hair preserved under glass in the collection of a steel magnate. Personally, I am thankful that the builders of McGill were North Britons and Presbyterians. The influence of Calvin and Knox blunted their aesthetic sense, but at least it saved them from the temptation of trying to blend the Middle Ages with the Industrial Revolution.

McGill's beauty must be discovered by living with it, for it grew out of her location and out of a character moulded by years of life in Montreal. It is un-selfconscious. Plain inside and out, the buildings on the main campus were constructed by thrifty men. Only the library is new, and in keeping with the tradition it is a long, low structure in the contemporary style with vast windows flooding the reading rooms with light. The older buildings are made of brick or Quebec gray stone. They are softened by no flower gardens, embellished by few ornaments, and in certain weathers they can look as gray as Edinburgh in an east wind.

So they should. For if Quebec is the enduring French Fact in America, this university, first in the Commonwealth to be granted a charter outside the home islands, is the most valuable enduring product of the Scottish Fact embedded in the core of Quebec since Wolfe's Highlanders stormed the Citadel. The French and the Scots have always understood each other. A Scot who married a *Canadienne* founded the university and gave her his name, and much of his wealth came from the fur trade which the Scots and French-Canadians developed to its highest point in the last decades of the eighteenth century and the early years of the nineteenth. The fur trade, more than any other single economic factor, made possible the existence of Canada as a nation.

From her rugged founder, practical yet imbued with a Scottish yearning for education, McGill's mature character has departed less than one might think. As James McGill's life was wedded to Montreal, so is that of his college. And if the University has done a little toward civilizing the city, the city has done even more toward

The Roddick Gates

broadening the mind of the academy.

On account of Montreal, this university has learned the value of many things which dons are apt to neglect because they are too obvious to seem interesting, and the chief of them is a sense of proportion. McGill men seldom make the error of overestimating the influence of themselves in a commercial and industrial society. If McGill lacks intellectual arrogance, it is because Montreal is unimpressed by intellectual attainments. If she is tolerant, it is because no intolerant organism could thrive, or even exist, in company with the amiable cynicism with which Montreal regards the affairs of mice and men. McGill is blessedly free of the twin curses of the modern academy: donnish preciousness and the hypocrisy imposed on so many New World universities by puritans who cannot understand the nature of the soil out of which the best roses grow. If Catullus returned to us, I would not guarantee that a large proportion of the Faculty Club could tell him honestly that they were acquainted with his poetry, but they would at least be able to entertain him without embarrassment. They would certainly understand what a poet needs before, during and after his dinner and would be happy and able to provide him with it.

But I was talking of McGill's beauty. It comes, as I said, from her location and character. Once you see it, it can be dramatic.

For this campus containing no single lovely building is a unit of surprising order in the chaos of the surrounding metropolis. It is an island of quiet in the city's roar, and at night an island of darkness in the city's blaze. Seen from Sherbrooke Street, the city's main artery which bounds the campus to the south, the buildings of McGill appear to grow right out of Mount Royal itself. Just above them are visible the roofs of Royal Victoria Hospital – long connected with the University's Medical School – the tower of the Allan Memorial and the tower of the civic reservoir. But high above them all – green in the spring, reddish-brown in the fall, brownish-white in the winter – is Montreal's wonderful mountain with its huge lighted cross, reminiscent of Maisonneuve, flaring eastward to what often is called the French end of town. Squirrels and pheasants live on the Mountain and even in the depths of winter you see them. Once in January I saw a pheasant pecking at the putty in the glass of a classroom window.

The appearance of this campus changes dramatically with the

violence of the Canadian seasons.

In summer McGill is as softly green as a cathedral close painted by Constable, the smoke-softened gray of the buildings almost buried under a wealth of elms. But the students in session never see it like this. When they arrive in the fall the leaves are already beginning to fall; when they finish their exams in the spring they are not yet out of the bud. For most of the academic year the campus is under snow, the elms as bare as brooms, the air far too cold for loitering. Men in later life remembering their student days here cannot easily think of moonlight and never can think of roses or may blossoms or the bibulous laughter of happy youth on a shadowed stream. More probably they recall heels creaking on packed snow, breath puffing out into arctic air, hands clasped against cold ears, the city shining in a frigid night, the Mountain crouched against the sky with the Bear and the North Star above it.

Always the graduate will remember McGill as an integral part of Montreal itself. The fraternity houses, even Royal Victoria College, are on the fringes of one of the busiest parts of the whole city. Traffic pounds past them, and no McGill student can possibly think of his university as a refuge from life. The city to which she is married is too big, too impinging, too violent in its greedy growth ever to let the university dream. And in this fact are hidden assets.

The staff members, making so many of their friendships in the city, do not easily become ingrown, and a student must be singularly stupid if he fails to see the connection between his studies and the life around him. The law students are within walking distance of the courts and law offices of Canada's largest city. The medical student is even closer to the hospitals which have made Montreal famous, from Osler's day to ours, as a medical centre of the world. Hundreds of neophyte engineers obtain their summer employment within a few miles of the classrooms where they receive their training.

Even the arts gain from their close association with a city like Montreal. A young philosopher studying Plato, a young theologian brooding over the message of St. Paul, a young poet immersed in Shakespeare can hardly succumb to the fallacy that saints, philosophers and poets are retiring persons who do their best work in seclusion. The raw materials of sainthood, poetry and philosophy, their very *raison d'être*, lie all around the student at McGill.

They seem to me quite as important to education as do the great books and the laboratories where thinkers and scientists seek to make their small contributions to order in a world which was and always will be rapacious, dangerous, exciting and alive.

When James McGill bequeathed his Burnside Estate for a college, Montreal was a small town on the river bank several miles below his property. If the rugged old man could have known that one day the city would entirely surround his university, I don't think he would have been sorry. James McGill was an extremely practical Scot who loved Montreal and enjoyed seeing her grow. What could have pleased him more than the thought that his university should become the city's geographical heart?

The Royal Victoria College

II

THE ORIGINS OF McGILL

BY HUGH MacLELLAN

CANADA is a country where most of the outlines are bold, rough and gigantic; it is also one where many of the details, perhaps in contrast to the grandeur of the environment, often seem startlingly petty. This country has tended to grow in surges. In the growing periods we find men of action, singularly inarticulate, almost literally taking some fragment of the huge landscape into their hands and shaking it. But each of these surges of growth has been followed by a time of hesitations during which men with the gift of leadership have been half paralyzed by the apathy of those around them.

The early story of McGill University – it goes back much further than the granting of the Charter in 1821 – falls into two of these contrasting epochs and perfectly illustrates the maniac-depressive character of Canadian history. The Founder lived in a time of heroic growth. The executors of his estate tried to realize his aims in one of the slackest and most discouraging periods the country ever knew.

The original Canadians – French, Scots and United Empire Loyalists – were all casualties of late eighteenth century history, and each of these groups faced challenges so severe they were nearly extinguished by them. The French-Canadians were the chief victims of France's loss of the Seven Years' War, the Scots of the destruction of the clan system in their native Highlands, the Loyalists of the collapse of British arms and statesmanship in the American Revolution. When these three splinter groups first encountered each other in Canada they had nothing in common but the land

James McGill

they were permitted to occupy and a deep-seated knowledge of what it feels like to have been totally defeated.

In Montreal toward the end of the eighteenth century, representatives of all these three groups met, did business and even to some extent intermarried. In their struggle for individual survival they established the necessary civic institutions to make Montreal a workable municipality. They acquired new points of view and an understanding of the importance of tact in a town of different races, creeds and languages. Fur was almost the only profitable commodity in the country, and many of the immigrant Scots joined the trade the French had long ago developed. It was a trade which had from the beginning a value far beyond any shown on a balance sheet, for the voyageurs searching for furs discovered and mapped the Mississippi Valley, and later were to discover and map the whole northwest of the continent. But civic progress was extremely slow, and the political future of British North America was dark. If it had not been for the astounding energy of a small group of great men, the Canadian nation would never have existed, for the people who made it would have been absorbed by the triumphant United States.

One of these early leaders was McGill's founder, and to a degree which can only be described as uncanny, this man's life reflects every important aspect of the confused and explosive period in which the prime elements of the Canadian nation were blown out of their original contexts and thrown together in the New World.

James McGill was born in Glasgow in 1744, the son of a hammerman, as a blacksmith or worker in wrought iron was called in Scotland then. The year after his birth the battle of Culloden was fought, and his uncle Robert served on the losing side. The battle, one of the saddest in British history, was to have a profound effect on the nation now called Canada and on James McGill himself. The Highlands never recovered from Culloden, nor did Scotland's quasi-independence of the English. The glens were occupied, the clan system was destroyed, and for years the whole country seethed with suspicion and bitterness. But what was Scotland's loss was to be Canada's gain, for in the generation after Culloden the first Scots immigrants began to enter Canada. Some came on their own initiative, others remained along the St. Lawrence after being disbanded from the Highland regiments which had served under

Wolfe, and these first comers were to be followed by so many more that Canada can almost be called a Franco-Scottish colony.

One of these immigrants was James McGill. He was not a Highlander and so far as we know, his father was not politically suspect, but the fact that he left Glasgow University without a degree shortly after entering it at the age of twelve proves that for the McGill family times were very bad. At any rate his father could see no future for his son in Scotland. James was barely in his teens when he left home in company with his younger brother John. Legend has it that the boys went to relatives in North Carolina, but all we know for sure is that they went to some place in the Thirteen Colonies.

Meanwhile the last of the great colonial wars broke out between France and Great Britain, with results fateful and permanent for Canada and the McGill family. Quebec fell to Wolfe in 1759, and in 1763, under the terms of the Peace of Paris, New France was ceded to Great Britain and became a British province.

For the French-Canadians this conquest was a traumatic experience from which their descendants have not yet entirely recovered. They were amputated from their motherland, their civil and military leaders were recalled to France, and had it not been for their clergy, who remained to preserve *le fait Français en Amerique*, they would have been leaderless and alone in a hostile, English-speaking Protestant continent. Their past history had been a great one and they knew it, but their future was desperate.

No ecclesiastical leadership, no matter how determined and skilful, can compensate for a total absence of leadership in civic and governmental affairs. After the Peace of Paris there was a vacuum in Quebec inviting the enterprise of any newcomer who aspired to fill it. The political vacuum was only partially filled by British governors appointed in London – only partially, because by the French they were not regarded as leaders but as masters. Had it not been for the development of a trade which the French could share with other non-French citizens, French-Canada would have acquired indefinitely the mentality of an occupied country.

Fortunately there were citizens at that time who liked the French and could work with them and at times even lead them. These were the newly arrived Scottish immigrants who, like the French themselves, were no strangers to the aftermaths of defeat in

Entrance to The Old Medical Building

war. One of these Scots was James McGill.

Now that New France had become a British province, its commercial opportunities were thrown open to all British subjects, and in the fur trade young McGill saw a chance for himself. At the age of nineteen he arrived in Montreal to look around. Other Scots were doing the same. Some, like Simon McTavish who was to become an associate of McGill, were thinking in terms of forming commercial companies. Others, like the Highland soldiers disbanded from the regiments, were marrying *Canadiennes* and were offering their brawny bodies for service in the canoe brigades of the fur trade.

The Canadian fur trade at that time was probably the hardest in which free men ever engaged, and some of the feats on the rivers astound the modern imagination. The voyageurs paddled all day at the average rate of forty strokes to the minute, and over the portages they had to carry both their canoes and their trade goods on their backs. Some of their leaders were also exploring the land for a Northwest Passage, and before James McGill's career was over, no less than four Canadian parties had paddled all the way across the continent and through the Rockies to the Pacific Ocean, and one party led by Alexander Mackenzie had voyaged from Fort Chipweyan down the Slave River, across Great Slave Lake and down *la grande rivière en bas* (which now bears his name) to the Beaufort Sea.

James McGill does not belong in the front rank of these voyageurs: he was no Peter Pond, no Mackenzie, Thompson or Fraser. But for a considerable period in his early life he lived as hard as any of them, and he learned the fur trade from the bottom of a canoe to the head office in Montreal. He was one of the nineteen founding members of the Beaver Club. As early as 1767 he was trading into Michilimackinac and in 1770 he went still further west in a canoe brigade. During this period he lived on salt pork and dried beans, he paddled and portaged and slept in the open on the ground. In the winter of 1771-1772 he even wintered on the Crow Wing River, a stream which enters the Mississippi from the west above the falls St Antony, and at that time was about as far west as any of the regular trading brigades ventured.

But McGill was neither by nature nor ambition an explorer; he was a burgher essentially, and as soon as he had rolled up a sufficient stake, he quit the rivers and settled in Montreal. He entered into a partnership with one Isaac Todd, and both he and Todd owned shares in Simon McTavish's North West Company. In Montreal, Todd & McGill were middlemen receiving the pelts from the canoes returning from the west, shipping them to England, and receiving from England the goods necessary to keep the trade alive. They prospered. Late in 1776 McGill married a Frenchwoman, the widow (with four children) of one Joseph Amable Trottier Desrivières, and it was about this time that he acquired the Maison de Bécancourt, located in the heart of the city close to the Chateau de Ramezay.

Meanwhile the third of the historical explosions decisive for Canadian history occurred – the American Revolution. James McGill was instantly affected by it, for he was among a band of Montreal merchants who formed a small militia unit to defend the city. The city was invaded nonetheless, and for a while Benjamin Franklin sat in the Chateau de Ramezay soliciting the Canadians to join the revolution. McGill was one of the leaders who kept Canada in the British camp, and shortly after Franklin had gone home baffled, the American troops retired and Montreal remained in British hands for the remainder of the war.

Whether American success in the Revolution decided McGill to sell his shares in the North West Company is uncertain, but it can hardly be unconnected with the fact that he did so in 1784. McGill had always favoured the Ohio territory and had never had the vision of McTavish who was convinced that the distant Athabasca region promised more. Now the Ohio was in American hands, and McGill did not for a moment believe that the Americans would permit Canadians to trade there freely. Though he never lost his interest in fur, he began to widen his activities into fields less adventurous.

Now in the full tide of his life, James McGill became a leader in every important activity in the growing city of Montreal. Steadily the public service began to occupy more of his time. In the year he withdrew from the North West Company he became a member of the 'Canadian' committee which prepared a petition to the King for an independent constitution, and thereby established his right to be considered a forerunner in the struggle for responsible government which was to occupy the best minds of Canada during the first half of the next century. In 1786 he organized the Montreal

The Principal's Residence

Fire Club to combat the fires which so often broke out among the warehouses and business properties. In 1787 he was appointed a major in the Montreal militia. In 1792 he was made an honorary member of the Executive Council of the Province, and in the same year he was elected by acclamation to the first parliament of Lower Canada. In 1793 he became a regular member of the Council.

McGill's military rank kept pace with his rise in civil life. In 1811 he was made a colonel of militia, and the next year at the beginning of the War of 1812 he was appointed Brigadier-General in charge of the garrison entrusted with the defence of Montreal. His rank soon became that of acting Major-General, and it was his unpleasant duty to negotiate with the Americans for the surrender of his city. Even now McGill's personal success was modified, as it had been modified all through his life, by the historical calamities in which he became involved.

But his personal success was immense and rather amazing. In his last years the son of the Glasgow hammerman was the leading citizen in a community of about 15,000 people located on one of the strategic cross-roads of the world, a community far more important than its size indicated. Living on the Burnside Estate which he had acquired in 1798, looking down the slope of farmland to the city where he had made his modest fortune, McGill must often have contemplated the past with wonder. He had indeed travelled a long and rough road from the little house in Stockwell Street in Glasgow where he had been born, and if the pictures we have of him are faithful, his appearance showed it. He was tall and portly and his grave demeanour had earned him the nickname of The Prior. His complexion was in a Scottish way florid, his eyes small and shrewd, his expression that of a stubborn and experienced old boar, yet withal kindly, and with some of the ruefulness many experienced Scots have, understanding how hard it is to be human, but how especially hard it is to be a Scot.

James McGill had always been a reader, and perhaps he guessed from the signs that the pioneering days were over in the Montreal district and that if history were any guide, the future would require a different type of man from the great adventurers with whom he had passed his own life. He was a realist, and about Montreal he had few illusions. He knew it would be improper to call the city even an outpost of civilization. Lusty and vigorous it was, and al-

35

The Three Graces

ready it had proved its capacity to survive and grow in a savagely difficult climate and terrain in a period of history when almost everything seemed to go against it. But civilized it was not – not yet – and as early as 1787 McGill himself had taken the measure of its culture.

A petition which he wrote, and which many of his fellow citizens signed, contained these telling words: 'We hardly know of a single school in any part of the district for teaching boys. Only one boy in five can read and write'.

The Home Government of Great Britain at that time still regarded Quebec more or less as an occupied country, assuming that its chief duties were to keep order and to protect the province from invasion. Since the Peace of Paris the *status quo* had been reasonably satisfactory and the government was loath to do anything to upset it. Faced with this demand for creating educational facilities, the authorities were cautious.

But the agitation for schools mounted, and in 1801 the government decided to make some kind of gesture to the reformers. It created The Royal Institution for the Advancement of Learning, of which McGill University today is the direct inheritor.

It would be wrong to assume that the motive of the government in inventing this magnificent title was a cynical one, but James McGill was not fooled by it for an instant. He knew it was no more than a gesture to appease men like himself. He knew also that there was opposition within the community to the Royal Institution ever becoming a reality, and that there were many in high places who were opposed to offering education to the poorer classes. He was not ignorant of the ways of governments, and he understood that it is their nature to temporize. The Royal Institution, existing solely on paper, was a convenient device to which the buck could be passed whenever the reformers called for action. But it was not a body that could do anything practical because the government had been careful to prevent it from becoming a body in any sense of the word; the government, in short, had omitted to provide the Royal Institution with flesh and blood trustees.

On March 8, 1811, the character of the government of Montreal and the unreality of the Royal Institution was in the forefront of James McGill's mind when he performed the most important act of his life and wrote his will. He deliberately framed that document

The Oldest Doorway

so that it might be used by his executors as a goad to stir the community and the authorities to action. To the Royal Institution he bequeathed in trust the sum of £10,000 together with his Burnside Estate of forty-six acres, the dwelling house and other buildings, for the erection on the estate and the endowment of a university or college. He made only two stipulations: one of the colleges must be called after himself and the University must be established within ten years of his death. In the event these conditions should not be fulfilled, the bequest was to revert to his other heirs within the family of his widow.

This will was prescient, as future developments were going to prove. Had it not been for the time-clause, there can be no doubt that the authorities would have dawdled indefinitely and that the University might never have been established at all.

James McGill's life was now almost over, and he died less than two years later at the end of 1813. He was buried in the old Protestant Cemetery and his tomb stood there until 1875, when it was removed and placed on the campus, before the steps of the Arts Building, where it is now. His had been a life in which the years of peace had been so few he must have found it hard to recall them. He had been in his cradle when Scotland was torn by the disastrous rebellion of Charles Edward Stuart; he had been in his teens when Canada was conquered by Wolfe and ceded to Great Britain; he had seen how the French Revolution had turned Quebec emotionally against France; he had lived through the Napoleonic Wars and now in the last year of his life but one he had seen his new country again suffering an invasion in which he himself had been forced to play a role intensely distasteful. Before he died in 1813 he at least had the satisfaction of seeing American armies everywhere repelled and the threat to Canada recede.

James McGill's death virtually coincided with the passing of the epic period in Canadian history. Exhausted by its long series of challenges, the country now entered a time of slack water, and it is perhaps fortunate that James McGill did not live long enough to see with his own eyes how slack and stagnant that water was to be.

It is doubtful if any great university in the world ever began its existence in circumstances more undignified than those that beset McGill. On the one hand the Royal Institution still lacked trustees and was therefore powerless to accept the bequest. On the other the family of James McGill's widow, led by one Francis Desrivières, had conceived the hope that if they ignored the will and clung to the property, the indolence of the authorities could be depended upon to do nothing to oust them, with the result that the time limit would lapse and the money and lands would revert to themselves. McGill was a shrewd man, but some flaw in his judgment – probably it sprang from native clannishness – had caused him gravely to miscalculate the character of his wife's nephew. Francis Desrivières was to prove himself as tenacious as any Norman peasant in French literature, an ideal type for survival in the spiritless atmosphere which developed in Montreal after McGill's death. Had it not been for the energy of a single man, the property would never have been acquired and the university would never have existed.

But the executors were fortunate in possessing a powerful and devoted spokesman in the person of Dr. John (later Bishop) Strachan, and McGill owes more to him than to any of its principals before Sir William Dawson. Strachan immediately set to work on the authorities, and though he could get nothing out of them until the wars ended, the year after Waterloo (April 9, 1816) he finally pressed them into making the Royal Institution a reality. Now, fifteen years after they had established the Royal Institution, the authorities provided it with a 'Body Corporate for the Advancement of Learning': in other words, with a board capable of doing business, signing documents and accepting James McGill's bequest. Some measure of the gentlemen's energy can be acquired from the fact that four years passed before they got around to making a formal claim to the money.

The situation now became fascinatingly squalid. During all the years after James McGill's death the Burnside House had been occupied by Francis Desrivières, who was also in control of the lands, products and rents of the Estate. He had never been so comfortable in his life. Knowing the terms of the will, also being fully cognizant of what can be accomplished in Montreal through artful delays, Desrivières calculated that if he could hang on for another three years the benefactor's bequest would be rendered null and void. So he hedged, he wrote evasive letters to the executors, and his character stood firm against any of Dr. Strachan's suggestions that his behaviour could be construed as ungrateful to the great man to whom he personally owed so much. Regretfully Dr. Strachan concluded that his only course was to urge the Board to go to law in order to oust Desrivières, and in the fall of 1820 they entered the courts. There they were to remain for the next fifteen years, for Desrivières, silent and impervious, dug in his heels and stayed put.

This turn of events was distressing to Dr. Strachan; it was distressing to quite a few people in Montreal. But a cynic might have found within it certain compensations. The Board of the Royal Institution for the Advancement of Learning could not by the wildest flatterer have been described as energetic, but now the behaviour of Desrivières so infuriated them that they were determined to get the better of him. In order to do so they must implement as many of the terms of the will as they could. Though they could not possess themselves of the property and the endowment until the court case was decided in their favour, they could at least go through the motions of setting up a university. Accordingly in the spring of 1821 they obtained from King William IV a charter for the University. In 1824 they went further: they appointed a Principal and four professors. It is true that the Principal had no college over which to preside and the professors had no students to teach, but their appointment was of value in the legal battle against Desrivières. The first Principal of McGill was, moreover, a considerable personality in his own right. He was the Reverend George Jehosophat Mountain, a man of formidable character and melancholy countenance, who later became Anglican Bishop of Quebec and lived, after the termination of his *faineant* principalship to intervene decisively in the quarrel which broke out between the governors and his successor. He also, five years after his own appointment in 1824, persuaded the Board to lay claim to the Burnside Property by conducting a formal opening of the University.

It is this opening on June 24, 1829, that most people take as the birthday of McGill; others claim the University was born when the Charter was granted in 1821. In any but the strictly legal sense the earlier date counts for nothing – no semblance of a university existed in 1821 – but the later date stands for quite a lot. After the

George Jehosophat Mountain

ceremonies of the formal opening were over, the Board met with the Montreal Medical Institution, which had been established in 1823, and came to an arrangement that they be engrafted to the University as a Faculty of Medicine, with one doctor a professor and the rest lecturers. Medicine was then being taught in the old General Hospital, and therefore it can be argued that teaching at McGill dates from June in 1829. It can also be claimed beyond any argument whatever that Medicine is the senior faculty within McGill University today.

As for the ceremonies surrounding this formal opening of McGill, it is a pity that Anthony Trollope was not on hand to record them. The Burnside Estate was now in considerable disrepair, for it had not escaped the notice of Mr. Desrivières' frugal mind that the chances were becoming more and more likely that one of these days he would be ousted. He had accordingly spent no money to keep the property up, with the result that his beasts were annoying the neighbours by roaming through the dilapidated fences and rooting in their gardens. Everything about Burnside was shabby when the ceremony of opening McGill occurred. Lacking Trollope for a witness, we must have recourse to a reporter on the Montreal *Gazette*.

The procession to Burnside, noted the *Gazette*, lacked 'the gaudy appearance and display of religious and Masonic processions, yet to the mind of the philosopher and friend of education it was simple and appropriate'. A large room in a house on the estate was fitted up, and the *Gazette* informs us that 'soon after one o'clock it was filled by the numerous and respectable individuals who had assembled to witness the ceremony'. The *Gazette* (it has always been a tactful newspaper since it severed its connections with Benjamin Franklin) does not mention what Francis Desrivières was doing while the speeches were made and the Principal read a prayer nearly two thousand words long. It did not have to. Its editor knew perfectly well that Mr. Desrivières would remain unmoved. After the ceremony was over, after McGill University had been formally opened. Desrivières was still in possession of Burnside House, the case was still in the courts, the monies were still not forthcoming, the professors and the Principal were still without their pay.

Six more years passed, and it was not until the February of 1835 that the case against Desrivières was settled by a formal decision of

John Bethune

the Judicial Committee of the Privy Council in London. Principal Mountain thereupon resigned and went for a time to England and the Board appointed another clergyman to succeed him, the Reverend S. J. Lockhart, who seems to have accepted the post but never undertaken any of its duties. On November 18 of that year the Board appointed still another man of the cloth, the Reverend John Bethune, who was Rector of Christ Church and who lacked (as Mr. Gladstone in his capacity of Colonial Secretary was later to point out) a college degree. Still Francis Desrivières refused to vacate the premises, and another two years were to pass before he finally did so. He therefore emerges out of this period as a man of real ability. At no great cost he maintained himself in the enjoyment of James McGill's property for almost a quarter of a century.

Now, at last, it seemed possible to make the Founder's dream a real thing. The lawsuits were over, the land, buildings and endowment were in the hands of the Board and the Governors, and a new Principal was in office. But there had been so many delays, so much acrimony, the government was so unwilling to help the bequest with additional funds, and Dr. Bethune's character – it shows in his face no less than in his actions – was not a fortunate one. Neither was his Principalship.

During this man's incumbency appears every vice of pettiness so often associated with educational history. The Principal quarrelled with the Board, the Board with the Governors, and had it not been for a general anxiety that Mr. Desrivières would go to law once more on the grounds that the Founder's will was not being implemented, nothing would have been done to erect even one building for the use of students. Plans were made and abandoned, plans were made and studied, and finally one plan for a building was made and accepted. Meanwhile the gentlemen wrangled. The Board decided that it could afford only three professorships – Classical Literature, Mathematics and Natural Philosophy, Metaphysical and Moral Philosophy – and that one of these professors should be the Principal himself. The Principal – at least so Mr. Gladstone seems to have believed – was unqualified to teach any of these subjects on a university level. He was also in a state of extreme and justifiable vexation against his Board. He had paid for the repair of the fences out of his own pocket, had sent them the bill, and now the Board was refusing to honour it and was telling him to reimburse himself out of the products of the farm. Meanwhile the fight between the Board and the Governors was being conducted with intensity, and it continued until 1842, when the Board finally yielded to the extent of preparing the documents necessary for the transfer of the Estate to the possession of the Governors. At the same time they so arranged the wording that they, the Board, still remained in essential control. But something at least was accomplished during the Principalship of Mr. Bethune. On September 6, 1843, a building was opened and instruction began.

Parturiunt montes – after James McGill's vision, after thirty years of delays, bickerings and plans, McGill University (the University proper as distinct from the Medical Faculty) began with an enrolment of twenty students.

Meanwhile the character of the Board, combined with the character of the Principal, had created a situation so intolerable that the Colonial Secretary, pressed by Bishop Mountain, decided that it was his duty to intervene. Mr. Gladstone gave it as his opinion that Principal Bethune must go, and he went. He was succeeded by one Edmund A. Meredith, who at least had the recommendation of being a university graduate (Trinity College, Dublin) and whose incumbency officially began in 1846, and officially terminated in 1853.

Mr. Meredith seems to have been more interested in his law practice than in the institution over which it is his sole distinction to have presided. Mr. Bethune had left him with a University containing an enrolment of some twenty students; when Meredith retired the enrolment had fallen to thirteen. Even more embarrassing was the financial status under the third (or was he the fourth?) Principal, as was attested by the plight of the lecturer in French. Mr. Montier, after working for an entire academic year, complained that his total salary was only £2 14s., and when the Board received his complaint they reminded him that during this time he had, after all, enjoyed the use of a cow and a garden.

On Meredith's retirement the University had no Principal, and came under the guidance of the Professor of Classics, Vice-Principal the Venerable Archdeacon Leach, who was to prove himself a considerable man and to serve the University for many years under circumstances much happier.

By this time the public of Montreal had become annoyed by the

kind of people who were floundering in the footsteps of the great man ·
who had desired to give them a college. The Governors, it was
rumoured, were now desirous of finding abroad a man of mark to
succeed Principal Meredith; they were even considering a total re-
organization on the model of one of the senior universities of England. In August 1854 a local newspaper called the *Sun*, long since
defunct, fired a broadside:

'All we need are persons at the helm who will take *an active interest* in the progress and advancement of the Institution . . . It won't
do to sit idly down – to follow the dignified and majestic example of
Cambridge and Oxford. Montreal is not in England – it is in
Canada. We have a way of doing things for ourselves. It is not necessary in order rightly to accomplish an end to ask how they do it
"at home"; we can find out a mode ourselves. McGill College will
never be anything until some exertion is made by those who have
control of it. A languid indifference or a sickly half-dead interest
will never secure it to a permanency among the institutions of
the day.'

The Governors were probably uninfluenced by this outburst of
local opinion, but they had no suggestions of their own to make,
and when Sir Edmund Head, the Governor-General, was consulted by them, he startled them by proposing that they forget about
selecting a famous Englishman and look closer to home.

At that time the only province in British North America which
had made any real cultural advance was Nova Scotia. Closer to
England and Massachussetts than Upper or Lower Canada, with a
vigorous seaborne trade, Nova Scotia in those days was relatively
less provincial than it is now. Under the leadership of Joseph Howe
the Nova Scotians had ousted the Family Compact which still
stifled Montreal, and though they were conservative in their attit-
udes, they respected a man not for his position but for what he
made of it.

Urged by the Governor-General, the Governors of McGill pick-
ed a Nova Scotian to succeed Mr. Meredith as Principal. In Nova
Scotia's Pictou County, which up to the present has probably produced more able, disinterested men for its size than any other in
Canada, was a young man called William Dawson, who had lived
the hard and rugged life of a poor colonist of the period, yet had completed courses at Edinburgh University. In 1855 the Governors

offered him the Principalship of McGill, he accepted and began his duties in the autumn of that year.

How William Dawson turned a broken down farm into a great university is the subject of the next chapter of this book.

III

SIR WILLIAM DAWSON'S
PRINCIPALSHIP, 1855 - 1893
BY EDGAR COLLARD

S IR William Dawson has often been described as 'the man who made McGill'. The description is justified. Not only did he lead the university out of its shallows and its miseries, he deeply impressed his own philosophy of education upon it in the years of its early growth. Even after his death, McGill continued to develop in the directions he had planned, despite the efforts of his successor to remould it. To this day, after all the changes of the years, the impress of Dawson upon McGill remains.

For this reason a study of Sir William Dawson is of more than biographical interest. A key to understanding McGill University lies in his background and character.

It was not without misgiving that Dawson was appointed principal of McGill. The governors were 'both startled and disappointed' when he was recommended to them. They had consulted the Governor-General, Sir Edmund Head, a man of university connections and literary tastes. They had expected him 'to indicate some man of mark in England'. Instead, Sir Edmund urged them to choose as principal a young colonist in Nova Scotia. Few, if any, of the governors of McGill had even heard of him.

Yet McGill was at a stage in its history when the vigorous realism of a young colonist could break its doubts and hesitations. Dawson assured the university's growth by turning it away from Old World models and developing its practical usefulness in a colonial society. The power of his influence gave McGill an inclination toward scientific and professional studies which is still its outstanding characteristic.

Sir William Dawson

SIR WILLIAM DAWSON'S PRINCIPALSHIP

Dawson was a true colonist, a British American. He was born in Pictou, Nova Scotia, in 1820. Nine years earlier his father, James Dawson, had set out for Pictou from Banffshire. He, with three other young Scots, had gone on foot the one hundred and eighty miles to the Scottish port town of Greenock. It was a hard experience. One snowy night they almost froze to death while sleeping out on a hillside.

James Dawson reached Pictou with nothing but the proverbial guinea in his pocket. In this colonial town he took his place among the godly and the industrious. His life was one of mingled prosperity and misfortune, but always one of effort. Of his father William Dawson was to write that 'he impressed us with a respect for honest labour, and taught us to prefer any useful employment to mere amusement'. This was a most important lesson, as later events were to prove.

By the time William Dawson came to McGill as its principal, at the age of thirty-five, his only experience of the Old World had been two winter sessions at Edinburgh University, and one later visit. He held no university degree, not receiving his M.A. from Edinburgh until a year later.

His visits to the Old World had made him more than ever conscious of being a colonist. When he appeared before an English debating club, someone congratulated him on speaking English so well. 'Possibly he supposed my native tongue was Chippewa or Micmac!' was Dawson's comment.

He once visited his mother's old home at Lonerig. 'Standing on a rising ground,' he says, 'where a turn of the road gives a last view of the old homestead and the ridge on which it is built, I have attempted to realise the feelings which must have wrung hundreds of Scottish hearts transplanted from homes in the motherland to take root in the New World of the West.' Perhaps in nothing is the spirit of the native colonist better revealed than in this admission that he could only attempt to imagine how a British emigrant might feel on leaving the Old World.

The appointment of a colonist as principal of a colonial university was an unusual step. But it is doubtful if a 'man of mark' from an English university, such as the governors of McGill would have preferred, could have adapted himself readily to the conditions Dawson faced on his arrival in Montreal.

William Craig Baynes

SIR WILLIAM DAWSON'S PRINCIPALSHIP

In the last of his university addresses Dawson gave his memorable picture of McGill University, as he had first seen it in the autumn of 1855. The grounds were unfenced and pastured at will by herds of cattle. The buildings were unfinished, partly in ruin, standing amidst a wilderness of excavators' and masons' rubbish, overgrown by weeds and bushes. The access from the city was by a circuitous and ungraded cart track, almost impassable by night. His residence was to be in one of the ruined buildings, 'destitute of nearly every requisite of civilized life'.

All these desolate conditions, however, did not break his spirit, or turn his eyes in more agreeable directions. It was the very nature of a resourceful colonist to see hardships as opportunities. Speaking of the difficulties that faced him, Dawson was to say: "Yet, on this account, the position had its charms for a young man accustomed to hard work and to difficult undertakings'.

As the colonial principal of a colonial university, Dawson turned without grievance or distaste to the plain tasks before him. He himself carried the household supplies up to his residence (the campus was then so far out of town that the tradesmen refused to make deliveries). He himself laid out the walks and planted the trees. He himself indexed the first books for the library, and took, as the beginning of a museum, McGill's only geological specimen, a common fossil coral which the registrar had been keeping in a pigeon-hole of his desk. He himself was ready to teach as well as administer, and to give courses in almost any field until other teachers could be engaged.

If hard and varied work did not discourage him, neither did the university's penury. For several years he spent the whole of his principal's salary in improving the university, living meanwhile on money of his own. It was with the future that he was concerned. The difficulties of the present were only the means by which the future would be realized. As for McGill's past, this was a paralysis, partly induced by Old World dreams, from which he wished the university to be delivered.

Dawson's practical approach is seen in his realization that in a new country universities could not hope to flourish until more and better schools had been established. Higher education must languish in a vacuum without vigorous primary and secondary education. As he pointed out in his inaugural lecture as principal, the absence of an adequate system of schools meant that 'those who do enter on a college course often arrive too young, and with a too slender amount of previous education'. This meant that a colonial university was in danger of seeking support 'by descending to the level of the schools'. Nor was it enough for McGill to wait until social conditions changed, and better schools had come into existence. McGill must take the lead.

Here, again, his background proved to be useful. He had been appointed the first Superintendent of Education for Nova Scotia in 1850. For three years he had travelled about the colony, studying school conditions and convincing the people of the need of a teachers' college. He had concluded this work in Nova Scotia in 1853. Four years later, as Principal of McGill, he founded the McGill Normal School. In this pioneering work of Dawson's lies the origin of McGill's modern Institute of Education.

Though hoping for more and better students from an improved system of schools, Dawson realized that, for many years to come, McGill could not hope to offer her undergraduates the resources of larger, wealthier, and older universities. He was anxious that colonial students should not come to feel inferior and diffident, but should find advantages in a greater self-reliance. In education, as in other things, a man must look to himself for his true progress.

With this attitude towards learning Dawson was an extraordinarily invigorating influence at McGill. He taught self-reliance not only by word but by example. He himself had attained his place in the international world of science mostly by his own efforts.

At the age of twenty-two William Dawson had formed at Pictou a museum to prove that the coal-beds of Nova Scotia were not all of one type, as had been generally supposed, but should be separated into three distinct groups. He had also formed notable collections of birds, insects and molluscs, as well as a herbarium of native plants.

Dawson's progress in science astonished Sir Charles Lyell, the British geologist, when he visited Nova Scotia at this time. Sir Charles had been advised to seek out young William Dawson at Pictou. So great was Dawson's knowledge, even at the age of twenty-two, that he guided Sir Charles in his geological exploration of Nova Scotia. Sir Charles found himself concurring in important opinions about the colony's geology that Dawson had

The Redpath Museum

already formed; he accepted Dawson's opinions about matters he himself did not have time to investigate. Soon afterwards, under Lyell's sponsorship, Dawson began writing his first papers for the *Quarterly Journal* of the Geological Society of London.

Yet at the time of Lyell's visit in 1842 Dawson's formal education in science consisted only of a course in 'Natural Philosophy' at the Pictou Academy and a single winter session at Edinburgh University.

By the time he was appointed principal of McGill in 1855, Dawson had already established his reputation among scientists. It was Dawson's personal reputation that gave McGill its first international standing. He was elected president of both the American Association for the Advancement of Science and the British Association. At McGill, and as principal, he acted as host to meetings of both associations.

Yet this respected standing in the world of science had been achieved by a man who was largely self-educated. And his education was almost universal. He was not only a geologist but a paleontologist, a mineralogist, a botanist, a zoologist, an ethnologist, an archaeologist, an agronomist, as well as a linguist (especially in Hebrew) and a theologian. In all of these fields he wrote books and papers, and gave lectures, and in some of these fields he wrote text-books. He was also one of the pioneers in the use of the microscope as an aid to science.

He taught students no more inspiring lesson than that they must not regard their opportunities at McGill as being too limited for high achievement in their professions. An education was not, he would say, something to be received, but something to be achieved. Application, observation, determination – these were the marks of the educated man, rather than the forms and shows, the ease and opulence of academic amenities.

McGill might have no dreaming spires, no ancient gardens open to the moonlight. But it had all a New World might offer in a keen air, an open way, few obstructions of rank or class, and no chilling academic rule that nothing must ever be done for the first time.

In this philosophy of self-reliant work his own example at McGill was prodigious. With him all seasons were seasons for study. His summer vacations were spent in strenuous field work. He explored the geology of Canada, the United States, Europe and the Middle

East. He climbed mountains, dredged from barges, went on walking tours (geological map in hand). From this field work he would return to McGill in the autumn with his 'many weighty boxes' filled with specimens for the university's museum.

During the academic year, every moment was filled. He kept a tray of unclassified geological specimens on the window-sill of his office. In a spare moment he would turn to this tray and consider what these specimens might be. When he ordered a cab to attend some meeting downtown, he would not wait idly for the cab to arrive. He would put on his overcoat, seat himself at his desk, and work until the moment when the cab was at the door.

Dawson's view was that the only justified recreation is a change of employment. To learn the refreshment of turning from one task to another was to him 'essential to the highest usefulness and the highest enjoyment of life'. He urged his students not to sink into 'absolute repose' during the summer, but to carry on their studies. 'I have not in this been giving advice,' he would say, 'which I have been unwilling to take myself.'

An anecdote of Dawson's attitude towards work was told by Canon Jacob Ellegood, the rector of the Church of St. James the Apostle in Montreal. Canon Ellegood, a man of about Sir William Dawson's age, was an enthusiastic golfer. 'Sir William, in later years,' says Canon Ellegood, 'suffered from ill-health, and I suggested to Lady Dawson, one day, that she should encourage Sir William to play golf. I will never forget her look. 'Sir William play golf – Sir William play golf!' she said, with an air which meant, 'How could you suppose that so grave a person as Sir William could think of indulging in sport?'

Well indeed had James Dawson in Pictou impressed upon his son 'a respect for honest labour' and taught him 'to prefer any useful employment to mere amusement'. It was a philosophy of the time and place. Sir William Dawson used to recall that in Pictou, as in most colonial communities, respectability of character was most likely to be found among those with ambition enough to seek the dignity of self-support, while the idlers were likely to sink 'into a sort of heathenism and semibarbarianism'. In such a community hard work came near to being the dividing line between the decent and the degenerate; work was almost a way of salvation.

The same attitude was his when he addressed the students at

Redpath Hall

McGill. His theme for his University Lecture in 1863 was *Duties of Educated Young Men in British North America.*

The duty of young British Americans was to prove themselves to be educated by the vigour and usefulness of their work: 'First, then, I would say that our country expects of you that you should prepare yourselves thoroughly for and pursue earnestly and perseveringly, some useful walk in life . . . British America has no room in it for idlers. There is more than enough work for all . . .'.

As a colonist with this outlook, Dawson was particularly fitted to raise McGill out of its discouragement, and to inspire a dedicated energy. But his background proved suitable in still another way.

When he came to McGill he faced the commercial community with no sense of uneasiness or disapproval as something alien to his mood or understanding, or as menacing the spirit of academic studies. Work was for him the health-giving exercise of man's faculties, and among the useful types of work, trade and industry always stood high in his estimation.

He had carried on his own scientific studies in Nova Scotia in such intervals as he could spare from helping his father in his ventures as shipbuilder, as printer, and as shopkeeper. Dawson himself knew what it was to handle tools, to set type, and to sell goods across a counter.

In Montreal, as a university principal in a business community, he felt himself in no unfriendly isolation. On the contrary, he believed that McGill's location in the commercial metropolis of Canada should be reckoned among its chief advantages.

With this background and outlook, Principal Dawson saw that the growth of the university would lie in the new studies, rather than in the old – in science, rather than in literature. This did not mean that he brushed aside the older studies, or held them of little account. He himself had benefited from them, under the excellent clerical teachers of the old Pictou Academy. His own prose style was direct and vivid; his descriptive passages in such books as *Acadian Geology* are perhaps as fine as anything in the literature of Canadian science.

He was aware of his own debt to the traditional learning and paid his tribute to it. He preserved what there had been of the literary tradition in McGill's Faculty of Arts. He regretted that more students, on their way in the university, could not linger to take an Arts degree. At the very end of his principalship he admitted that there had been a want of balance in McGill's development. 'It is the academical faculty or Faculty of Arts,' he said, 'that is most in need.'

Despite these tributes to the humanist tradition, and his regrets that it had not flourished under him, Dawson was powerfully drawn away towards the scientific and the practical. That this should have been so, is partly explained by the practical experiences of his own life. But additional influences had formed his views.

He was stirred at beholding the rising dawn of a new scientific era, with all its excitements and wonders. This was a feeling he shared with many in the world of his day. But for him it had special meaning because he was set in a colony where science could accomplish the needed growth.

Dawson himself, in 1870, spoke frankly about the choices that had lain before him, in moulding McGill's character. He could have fallen back upon the traditional and limited curriculum of the English universities, with as much of university show, titles and ceremonies as McGill's limited means would allow.

This choice, he was convinced, would have ended in failure. It would be offering something, 'for which, however valuable, the palate of a new and young society has little relish . . . We had no mass of educated gentry trained in this method to support us'.

The alternative was to cherish whatever of the old learning had been already established at McGill, but to add the modern subjects, 'which by being more popular, and in some respects more practical, increase the value of the education given, and at the same time cause it to be more sought after'.

He felt that too great an emphasis on the old type of learning would give the university a reputation for being an impractical institution, and this would retard its expansion. In his inaugural address in 1855, after speaking of 'the large obligations that we owe to the literature of classical antiquity,' he warned of the 'danger that the time of students may be so occupied and their minds so filled with such studies that they may go from our colleges armed with an antique panoply more fitted for the cases of a museum than to appear in the walks of actual life . . . there can be no question that the wide-spread dissatisfaction arising from this cause, and from the apparent want of applicability of collegiate studies to the ordinary pursuits of life, has been largely influential in withdrawing public sympathy and support from the higher institutions of learning'.

Though placing the emphasis on practical learning, Dawson had to work with persistence and patience before McGill's growth was evident or impressive.

It was his conviction, however, that 'progress would inspire hope'. It was important to move back to the abandoned campus, to give outward signs of life and action. He was determined that as soon as the number of students in Arts exceeded fifty, they should leave the quarters in the High School (to which the faculty had retreated in 1852) and should reoccupy the dilapidated Arts Building on the campus.

This was done in 1860. And William Molson was inspired by this move to complete the building. He erected a West Wing to provide a convocation hall and a library, as well as connecting sections (with useful classrooms) to make one building out of the three blocks.

Dawson's ultimate achievements were all the greater for the many frustrations he had to endure. While trying to attract support to the university by offering practical courses of study, he had repeatedly to admit defeat.

He established a School of Engineering. But this school, 'unaided by the public, was at length suspended owing to the temporary embarrassments of the university'. A chair of practical chemistry 'failed to attract our artisans or manufacturers to receive its benefits, and the same fate has befallen,' he said, 'my own efforts to bring the principles of Scientific Agriculture under the notice of our farmers'.

So far from being discouraged, he only waited for later opportunities. 'Some men may regard these efforts as failures,' he said in 1870. 'For my part I am not ashamed of them . . . There is not one of them which is not important for the material progress of the country; and there is not one of them which by us, or others, will not be at length successfully carried out. I do not yet despair of any of them.'

This confidence in the power of growth in practical studies, even in the face of his disappointments, gave his efforts the quality of

Peter Redpath

faith. Before the end of his principalship, that faith was richly justified.

In the last of his university addresses, before his retirement in 1893, he could speak of the changes taking place all about him, the very changes he had foreseen and attracted. Already, in the 1880's, Peter Redpath had built a museum of natural science (especially for the teaching of geology); it was one of the finest museum buildings in North America. In addition, early in the 1890's, Peter Redpath had added a splendid university library. Engineering was impressively represented by two new buildings, the Workman Building for Mechanical Engineering and the Macdonald Engineering Building. There was also the Macdonald Physics Building.

The growing reputation of the university in natural history and in the sciences of chemistry, engineering and physics, was greatly strengthened by the progress in medicine.

The Faculty of Medicine had always been the strongest in the university. Principal Dawson could say even when he came to McGill in 1855 that it was 'second to none in America.' In its origin, the faculty predated the university. It had been established in 1823 as a 'Seminar of Medical Learning,' under the name of the Montreal Medical Institution. It had been 'engrafted' upon the university in 1829, as its Medical Faculty.

From the first, its professors, Scotsmen of energy and ability, had modelled it after the Medical Faculty of Edinburgh, and provided (then a unique thing in North America) instruction for the students in the hospital wards. The coming of William Osler to McGill was to give the faculty a further impetus. But Osler chose to come to McGill from Ontario because of the high reputation the faculty already had, and the unusual advantages he could find there.

Osler was indebted not only to a number of his teachers – the Dean, Dr Palmer Howard, above all – but he found himself a student with a group of young men of intellectual power and promise. The importance of Osler in relation to McGill as student and, later, as teacher, was the outcome of an intricate combination of influences. It was the combination of what his teachers and fellow-students (and later his faculty colleagues) did for him in a community of extraordinary mental keenness and progress, and of the

legacy he left to McGill by his own example of industry and enterprise and zest – a legacy symbolized at the end by his choice of
McGill for his cherished library, where his ashes were brought to
rest, as in a homecoming.

The stirring of Osler's mind at McGill came about not only from
the spirit of medical progress in the faculty but in the general
interest in natural history in the university, the result of Principal
Dawson's influence.

An example of this influence is to be found in the Osler Library
at McGill, in a note in Osler's handwriting in his copy of Darwin's
paper *On the Tendency of Species to Form Varieties*. In this note Osler
describes a meeting with Charles Darwin at a scientific gathering
in England in 1874. 'He spoke much of Principal Dawson of Mc-
Gill,' Osler writes, 'for whose work in fossil botany he had a great
regard. I remember how pleased I was that he should have asked
after Dr Dawson.'

Though the Medical Faculty, by its very origin and early years,
had been largely separate from the university, Principal Dawson
gradually brought about a closer association. In the 1870's the
faculty left the building it had been using on Cote Street in the city,
and came back to the campus. It erected a building of its own,
where the Biological Building stands today.

Not only was medicine now represented on the campus itself;
Dawson himself was a very real point of contact, as the professor
who gave generations of medical students the courses in botany
and zoology. The charm and value of this teaching Osler himself
acknowledged with enthusiasm. 'What a rare man he was!' he
wrote to Dr Shepherd in after years, when they were both recalling
memories of the old days at McGill.

All this varied progress in science at McGill was rising like a tide
when Dawson came to the end of his principalship. This made his
leave-taking in 1893 both a triumph and a tragedy. It was a
triumph, because what he had believed and worked for was at last
coming to pass; it was a tragedy because he must leave at the very
time of fulfilment. 'While personally,' he said in his last university
address, 'it is necessarily a matter for regret that I cannot continue
in office till the great improvements . . . are realized, it is at least
something, after our long and arduous journey through the wilderness of penury and privation, to see afar off the goodly land into

The Biology Building

which my successors are entering . . .'

In looking back on his own work, he rightly appraised what its purpose and value had been. He had been the pioneer, ready and able to do the rough and hard work. His very Canadianism, his background of life under colonial conditions, had proved one of his greatest advantages. 'My function in this university has been that of the pioneer,' he said; 'and viewed in this light it has not been compatible with the dignity and authority which are usually attached to the heads of more firmly established colleges in older countries. It is time, however, that this should be changed, and my successor should enter upon office under more favourable conditions than those of the feeble and struggling university of the past.'

Dawson knew, as a pioneer, that he had brought great progress out of feeble beginnings, but he had not brought about proportioned growth. The limitations were real and serious. The rich cosmopolitan world of humanist culture had been comparatively neglected. Unfriendly critics might suggest that Principal Dawson had promoted the growth of McGill by shrewdly emphasizing materialistic aims in a materialistic society, and by offering the community only what it would be willing to pay for.

Yet there is far more subtlety and far more greatness in Dawson's mind and character than such an interpretation would suggest. Dawson did not believe that science invariably needed the humanist studies to fill its deficiencies. It was his belief that science itself could offer much of what humanist studies inspired: in a sense of wonder, in beauty, and in the enrichment of the spirit as well as the mind. He was convinced that the proper study of mankind was not so much man and the works of man, as God and the works of God.

This conviction resulted from the logic of his religion. Accepting, as he did, the theological dogma that man is a fallen creature, he believed that man's work must share the corruption of his nature. Would not the humanist studies, for that very reason, be tainted even at their best? How could man hope to raise himself through education if he were to steep his mind only in what must be discoloured by the sin of Adam?

Dawson questioned whether the arts of man could contribute to the highest development of mankind; they might even stand in the way of God's own influence. On a Sunday morning in 1874 he led a procession of some sixty-five members from Erskine Presbyterian Church in Montreal, in protest against the introduction of an organ. He then helped to found a new Presbyterian congregation – known as the Stanley Street Presbyterian Church – on the condition that so long as there might be a single dissenting voice, no organ would ever be introduced.

He explained and defended his viewpoint in a pamphlet, *Instrumental Music in Churches*. Art, he said, was a questionable aid to religion. The attention of the worshipper might become fixed upon music, rather than upon God. He would be pleased with what man had done, not with what God might do. A church service might become an entertainment. Such 'praising machines' as church organs might be quite as hollow as the 'praying machines' of Tibet.

This attitude towards the arts, as intrusions upon the worship or understanding of God, was also disclosed in his role as president of the Montreal Natural History Society. He took great interest in the Society's museum, as he believed that in a well-ordered museum the handiwork of God could be the most impressively displayed. At some time, however, a gift had been made to the Montreal Natural History Society of a plaster cast of the antique Greek statue of the Discobolus. To Dawson this must have seemed an intrusion of the works of man among the works of God. 'The world has worshipped art too much, reverenced nature too little,' he told the Society in 1856.

He could not reconcile himself to the art that sought not only to depict the thoughts of man's corrupt mind, but even the nakedness of man, when 'in our present fallen state, considerations, both moral and physical, require that the nakedness . . . should be covered from our sight'.

It is not surprising that when the English satirist, Samuel Butler, visited the museum of the Montreal Natural History Society in 1875 he found the Discobolus stored out of sight of the public in a dusty lumber-room with its face to the wall. In this room he also found an old man stuffing an owl; he was S. W. Passmore, taxidermist to the society. When he inquired why the Discobolus was not put on display, he was told by the old man that it was 'rather vulgar'.

In this incident originated Samuel Butler's celebrated poem,

The Macdonald Physics Building

SIR WILLIAM DAWSON'S PRINCIPALSHIP

A Psalm of Montreal :
  Stowed away in a Montreal lumber room
  The Discobolus standeth and turneth his face to the wall;
  Dusty, cobweb-covered, maimed and set at naught,
  Beauty crieth in an attic and no man regardeth:

                              O God! O Montreal!

Yet Principal Dawson was no Philistine, blaspheming beauty. He did not question the art of man, whether in the church organ or in the Greek statue, because it was beautiful; he questioned it because it was not beautiful enough. In choosing such man-made things the world had not chosen the better part. In contemplating the works of God (all save the human figure which man himself had debased) man might find sensuous enjoyment, free from the taint of his own imperfection.

To the Montreal Natural History Society he had expounded his philosophy of beauty. Of the world of nature he said: 'It was the pleasure, the show, the spectacle prepared for man in Eden, and how much true philosophy and taste shine in the simple words, that in that paradise, God planted trees 'pleasant to the sight' as well as 'good for food'; and other things being equal, the nearer we can return to this primitive taste, the greater will be our sensuous enjoyment, the better the influence of our pleasures on our moral nature, because they will then depend upon the cultivation of tastes at once natural and harmless, and will not lead us into communion with, and reverence for, merely human genius, but will conduct us into the presence of the infinite perfection of the Creator.'

Such a passage opens up the inner heart of Dawson's philosophy as an educator. He did not bring science to its dominant position at McGill only because it was a useful study which a practical community might support; he found in science the possibilities of the well-rounded education, at once spiritual and practical, as full of ministrations to man's love of beauty, as of applications to his daily work.

In this spirit he himself taught science throughout the years of his principalship. He taught it not as a cold and chilling thing dehumanizing the soul. He taught science as the study of the handiwork of God, a subject as sacred as it was practical. 'I may add here,' wrote Dawson in the year of his death, 'that, in so far as I have had any success as a teacher of Natural Science, it has been due to my reverent regard for every natural object, as the hand-work of God, and as consequently a sacred thing, the description and illustration of which was to supersede altogether any considera-tion of personal display or reputation'.

This religious attitude gave inner meaning not only to Dawson's emphasis on science at McGill but to the whole range of Dawson's work as principal.

McGill, by its charter, was non-sectarian. Of this Dawson heartily approved; he had seen much elsewhere of the baleful consequences of sectarian strife. But he strove, by his own influence, to prevent the non-sectarian university from becoming merely secular.

He set the religious example. Religious references were introduced into his university addresses. Every Sunday he was to be seen walk-ing down the campus, his Bible under his arm, to some neighbouring hall, to conduct his Bible classes. In the vast nineteenth century controversy between science and religion, he took the stand that the Bible had nothing to fear from science, as distinct from scientific speculation.

In a religious spirit he cared for the students. He arranged to have all the classes come in turn to gatherings at his residence in the East Wing, and in the course of the evening would give a little talk on the Bible and science. He let it be known that any student was welcome to call upon him at any time; he was known to leave his dining-table, that an anxious student might not have to wait. He would visit students if they were ill, and pay their fees if they were poor.

Dawson's presence may be felt before the portrait by Wyatt Eaton in the Redpath Museum. It is a commanding presence, but it commands by its beneficence. 'There was a certain impression of gentleness, simplicity and dignity made by his very presence on the campus,' a graduate recalls. 'Somehow I always had an in-stinctive reverence for his character.'

Another graduate writes: 'What impressed me most of all in regard to our revered principal was his noble type of personality. He was a man of fine physique and benign countenance and bore all the marks of a student and deep thinker. He was humble and approachable, though with a strength of character that command-ed your respect. It mattered not what sort of rumpus was in his

Redpath Hall

class before he arrived. All he had to do was to turn his eye to floor and gallery and there was order and respectful calm.'

If Dawson's religion explains his zeal for science, it explains also the quality of his administration. He believed that if a principal is to command respect – the respect he needs to carry out his duties – he must be the servant, not the master.

He contributed to a symposium on 'Discipline in American Colleges,' conducted by *The North American Review* in 1889. 'The instructor or administrator,' he said, 'must bear in mind that he also serves a Master, and is in some sense the servant of all, and that "the Lord's servant must not strive, but be gentle toward all, apt to teach, forbearing, in meekness correcting those that oppose themselves". If by God's grace he can serve in this manner, the question of control is not likely to arise in any very acute form.'

The question of control never did arise in any very acute form during Dawson's principalship. He was grateful at the end that in all his thirty-eight years in office there had been 'no serious breaches of discipline, no college emeutes or rebellions'. Yet the dignity with which he presided over McGill is repeatedly described in accounts of his time as 'deferential'. He had set an example of such hard and honest work, such self-denial, and such forbearance and kindliness that few could oppose him with any sense of satisfaction, even when they disagreed with his opinions.

Such a principal, while leading McGill along lines of practical usefulness, could also give it a sense of spiritual elevation in the study of science and consecrated exertion in the ordinary work of the world. With his death, however, the softening influence of his presence faded; his special vision of the religious quality of science lost its warmth; while the momentum he had given to professional and scientific studies increased as McGill entered into the industrial expansion of the Twentieth Century.

IV

SIR WILLIAM PETERSON'S
PRINCIPALSHIP, 1895 - 1919

BY EDGAR COLLARD

T H E choice of a successor to Sir William Dawson was one of the most difficult the governors of McGill University have ever had to make.

Sir William Dawson had almost created the university, and he had done so by his emphasis on science and the professions. Nothing should be done to retard the impetus he had given to McGill's growth. But a principal was now needed who would give the work in Arts a larger role than it had, or perhaps could have had, under the conditions of Dawson's time. What the governors needed in the new principal was a man who would be able to bring the scientific and the humanist traditions more closely together, and cause both to flourish in the university.

One superb possibility was considered. This was the appointment of Dr William Osler, then professor of clinical medicine at the University of Pennsylvania. Dr Osler was a graduate of McGill; he had been one of the medical professors; he had personal eminence to bring with him. No man, perhaps, could have done more to carry forward the success and reputation of McGill in science, while introducing his love of literature. In him the scientific and humanist traditions were joined; he might have succeeded in joining them in the university.

Dr Osler, however, declined the invitation to come back to McGill as principal. 'Executive work has never been in my line,' he said. The governors had to look elsewhere.

They looked where the governors had wished to look in 1855; they sought 'a man of mark' in the Old World. The chancellor,

Sir William Osler: The Young Physician

Lord Strathcona, played his part in the selection. Though a colonist for a great part of his life, Lord Strathcona was a Scot by birth, and a Scot who spent the greater part of his later years in the British Isles, with an estate at Glencoe. In William Peterson he chose a fellow-countryman.

The dramatic interest of Principal Peterson's work at McGill lies in its elements of conflict. He had many of the qualities and attainments that were needed. Yet his very achievements at McGill were to be clouded by misunderstandings and disappointments. Under his principalship McGill swept forward in a full tide of growth, while his own life became one of embittered sadness, almost deepening into personal tragedy.

The qualifications of William Peterson for his difficult position at McGill were impressive. Far more than Dawson, he was the academic personage, by training and instinct. Whereas Dawson had become principal without having a degree, and was mostly self-educated, Peterson was the product of some of the richest educational traditions of the Old World – a graduate in classics of Edinburgh and Oxford, and a student of Göttingen. The thoroughness of his classical knowledge and the grace of his translations had already earned him a respected place in the exacting world of international scholarship.

Nor was he the scholar only. He had command over the details and outlook of administration. As principal of University College in Dundee his executive ability had been proved. At McGill, in larger responsibilities, he often rose to the stature of an academic statesman.

In appearance and character he contrasted strikingly with his predecessor. He did not have Dawson's grave and attentive kindliness; he had, rather, the austerely clear lines of profile that would make a distinguished medallion. His dignity was of the type that bordered on *hauteur*. Though he had many of the Scottish traits of independence, these had been merged into a more sophisticated cosmopolitan culture.

No doubt the whole complex story of William Peterson's principalship at McGill existed in essence even before his principalship had begun. His years at McGill only unfolded an inevitable conflict. He was the right man for his position, and the wrong one; the rightness and the wrongness were both fully displayed before the end.

Sir William Peterson

In his intellect, Principal Peterson well analyzed what his position at McGill required. He said, wisely, that he had not come to disparage anything that his predecessor had achieved. He agreed that it was 'expedient in the past that the generosity of benefactors should be guided to flow in channels which have raised some of the other Faculties (other than the Faculty of Arts) to a level on which they may challenge comparison with similar institutions anywhere'.

He realized quite clearly that in coming to Montreal he was not coming to a city where the university would dominate all the life about it. He had come to the commercial metropolis of Canada, which had a university within it. He did not wish to set the university and commerce against each other; he wished to draw the two together, that each might enrich the other.

Nor was this enrichment to be merely the yielding up of commercial wealth for the support of university studies; it was to be a mingling of the wisdom that belonged to each. With conciliatory realism he delivered an address in Montreal on 'the Place of the University in a Commercial City'. He quoted the words he had heard from Principal Tulloch when he had begun his work at University College in Dundee.

Old Principal Tulloch had said: 'Nowhere does the school of life afford a better training in the qualities of prudence, good sense, sagacity, keeping your own counsel and doing your own work without too much fuss than in a thriving commercial community. No qualities can be more useful or wear better than these, and I fear it is possible to pass through any college, or even to teach in a college, without sometimes having a conspicuous share of them'.

No quotation could have sounded a note of more astute reconciliation. He did not believe, he said, that commerce and the humanities could advance by struggling to press each other aside. On the contrary, McGill should become a centre of practical usefulness in the community, but about that practical usefulness should be built 'higher elements of thought and sentiment and aspiration – literary, scientific, philosophical, artistic'.

He went further, saying: 'I hope you share my view that what a modern university has to offer in the midst of a commercial city, so far from disqualifying a man for success in business, ought to help him forward, just as is the case in the professions'.

In all this lay something far more than artful pretence. Principal

Lord Strathcona

Peterson was showing that masterly touch he truly possessed. If he had only been able to carry out in practice what he so soundly expounded in theory, his principalship might have amply fulfilled those requirements, exacting as they were, that had led to his appointment.

It was not long, however, before Principal Peterson had made many enemies in Montreal, but his most pertinacious enemy, from first to last, was himself. He encumbered his own path; he obstructed his own purposes. Nor is there reason to suppose that he ever felt regret – much less remorse – at the many difficulties he himself aroused.

Though he came with a scholar's devotion to minister to needs, he could not keep himself from scorning deficiencies. Sound and ample as his scholarship was, he had the pride of it. The haughtiness of his ministration could scarcely be received with gratitude. The greater tragedy of his life in Montreal was that he failed to win the fellowship in progress which he, in his mind, so clearly understood and expressed.

The manners of the middle-aged are never easily changed, and by the time of his appointment Peterson was already middle-aged. His tastes and habits had been formed. He was hesitant, even reluctant, to leave Scotland for Canada. Twice Lord Strathcona had to call upon him, before he could persuade him to accept the McGill principalship.

When his predecessor, William Dawson, came to Montreal as principal, he was coming to a city in which he had never set foot. But he was a British American, moving from one colony to another. He found conditions wanting in development, like those at home. Though in a new city, he was scarcely a stranger. The qualities of the pioneer were needed; these he could supply.

William Peterson, however, in moving from the Old World to Canada was moving from one world to another. From the land of his heart, oceans divided him and a waste of seas. He spoke of 'the feeling of strangeness' which marked his first days: he was 'a stranger addressing strangers'. More deeply, he described himself as 'one who had literally "torn himself up by the roots" from the position he had been honoured by holding in the home-country'.

The expression 'home-country' came repeatedly into his thoughts and into his words. Though nearly twenty-five years as principal

The Macdonald Engineering Building

of McGill, he never regarded himself as a Canadian. He was an educator from the home-country, serving faithfully in exile in a distant colony.

Every spring, as soon as the academic year at McGill ended, he would leave for the British Isles or for Europe. The affairs of the University, of course, made such visits at times necessary. But this was not always their real cause. He was going home to refresh his soul in the lands of ancient history and ripe learning. The dignity of university buildings graced by the Middle Ages, the riches of full libraries, the spirit of timeless scholarship without regard to the urgencies of the market-place – all these brought him back to himself.

When he returned to McGill in the autumn, he was like those other Britons who were sailing for posts of Empire, to do their duty. On his arrival in Montreal he would grant interviews with the newspapers and these interviews were seldom fortunate.

An interview with *The Gazette* in Montreal in September 1904, reads: 'Dr Peterson said that Hon. John Morley, one of the distinguished members of the Liberal party in England, was going to favour Montreal with a visit about the end of October, after his American trip, and then Montrealers would have an opportunity of showing the well-known statesman what was being done on the outskirts of the Empire, in Britain's chief colony'.

The impression of aloofness given by Principal Peterson was heightened when he sent his sons to the home-land for their education, and when his wife, unhappy in colonial society, spent little time in Montreal. As the years passed, the difficulties he faced or created deepened; his isolation within the university became more pronounced. Principal Dawson, mounting the steps of his residence in the old East Wing of the college, was part of McGill, and the light that shone from his study window was a kindly, welcoming light. Principal Peterson, walking down the campus avenue to his residence in the neighbouring Prince of Wales Terrace on Sherbrooke Street, was an austere figure entering into loneliness.

If the principalship of Sir William Peterson had been a failure, it would have had greater dramatic unity. The irony of his principalship was that it was an outstanding success. During his years at McGill the University prospered magnificently. But it prospered most in ways that were not nearest to his heart.

Principal Dawson had brought scientific prestige to McGill by his own standing in the world of science, and by the early impetus he gave to scientific interests in the university. But it was during Principal Peterson's principalship that McGill gained full stature as a scientific centre both in research and in teaching.

The row of new science buildings, in the style of late Victorian Renaissance, was being completed when he arrived as principal in 1895. In engineering, chemistry and physics McGill was to possess some of the newest and finest buildings and equipment on the continent.

Science found new prosperity in other ways. The Medical Faculty was given a splendid new building. And this building made accommodation not only for the increasing number of students coming to McGill but for the new laboratories and equipment that the broadening conception of medicine demanded.

The faculty of agriculture, which Principal Dawson had hoped to establish at McGill, was now set up on a new campus of nearly 800 acres some twenty miles away, at Ste. Anne-de-Bellevue. On these new grounds at Ste. Anne's a department of Household Science was also established. Thither, too, the School for Teachers was moved to pleasant new quarters, from the old building on Belmont Street, where Dawson had established the McGill Normal School in 1857.

The expansion of McGill's land was itself an outward sign of development. Times had changed wonderfully from the days when Principal Dawson, at his own expense, had tried to improve the abandoned campus in Montreal, in the hope that he might discourage the governors from selling more of it for building lots. In addition to the 800 new acres at Ste. Anne-de-Bellevue, McGill was given three old estates in Montreal close to the original campus – the Molson, Law and Frothingham estates. They comprised one of the last of the open areas left near the heart of the city, and gave the university land which, only today, is being completely brought into use.

Under Sir William Peterson's principalship new departments were established in music, social service, commerce, dentistry and physical education, as well as a school for graduate studies. The number of students more than doubled. The endowments, only about a million dollars when he came to McGill, rose to over twelve millions. The University's income rose from two hundred

The Macdonald Chemistry Building

thousand dollars to a million dollars.

Great as this expansion was, it was not quite of the kind that Principal Peterson had urged in his inaugural lecture, nor was it through such expansion that he could make his greatest contribution. As McGill's professor of classics, he had identified himself particularly with the Faculty of Arts. He had urged 'all intending benefactors' of the university to 'concentrate their attention' upon it. The Faculty of Arts was not only the most in need, it was the most worthy of support. 'We must strive after beauty as well as truth,' he had said at the beginning of his principalship.

Yet the benefactors of McGill under Sir William Peterson's principalship had almost passed by the Faculty of Arts to concentrate their attention on the sciences and the professions. Principal Dawson, as a scientist, had the satisfaction of seeing the university achieve in science its greatest success. But Principal Peterson, as a humanist, saw the university flourish elsewhere than in his cherished field. In this ironic way, he might feel that the very prosperity of McGill in his time was evidence of his frustration, even of his failure.

It is not often that the eulogy at a memorial service dwells upon the disappointments and failures of a man's life. But so it was with the address delivered in Montreal at the memorial service held for Sir William Peterson in 1921. The speaker was the Rev. Dr. D. J. Fraser, principal of the Presbyterian College affiliated with the university.

'I always detected in his life a certain undefined loneliness,' said Dr Fraser. 'The scholar's shyness and the isolation of his exalted position hardly account for it. A humanistic scholar in a university where the practical departments were making the greatest progress, engrossed in his intellectual interests in the solitude of his upper chamber while the busy commercial world went heedless by . . . an old countryman in a new land that he could never quite call "home," a controversialist skilled only in the use of the rapier and compelled at times to enter the lists with those who wielded the bludgeon . . . a lover of his own fireside who must of necessity be socially advertised with the vulgar, his spirit dwelt apart from the busy world in which he served'.

It is doubtful if the University would have expanded under Sir William Peterson if the giving of funds had had to depend upon the wide popularity or appeal of the principal. Fortunately, this was

Douglas Hall

not necessary. The funds for the sweeping expansion under his principalship came mostly from two benefactors – Sir William Macdonald, the Montreal tobacco merchant, and Lord Strathcona, one of the financiers of the Canadian Pacific Railway, governor of the Hudson's Bay Company, and president of the Bank of Montreal.

It was Sir William who gave the money for the new row of science buildings down the eastern side of the campus – the new buildings for engineering, chemistry and physics. It was he who gave the 800 acres at Ste. Anne-de-Bellevue and the three estates in Montreal. It was he who gave the funds to establish the Faculty of Agriculture and most of the new departments. Apart from the legacies in his will, his gifts to the university during his lifetime have been estimated at about eleven million dollars.

Lord Strathcona's benefactions were also many. Chief among these were the new medical building and the Royal Victoria College for women students.

With two such benefactors, Principal Peterson was not primarily dependent for the university's growth on public appeals. Nor was it he who had first attached these benefactors to McGill. This had been done by his predecessor, Principal Dawson. But Principal Peterson had certainly retained and deepened their interest in the university. This did not prove difficult in the case of Lord Strathcona. Not only did both have a Scots background but Principal Peterson was, very largely, Lord Strathcona's choice and protégé. As for Sir William Macdonald, there was the curious bond of mutual austerities, for Sir William, in his own very different way, was as aloof, and as lonely, as Principal Peterson.

In his relations with Montrealers generally, Principal Peterson was far less successful. Want of understanding between him and the community developed into misunderstanding. The result was a disturbing unpopularity.

The relations between the governors and the principal were at times unhappy – all the more unhappy because the principal had tended to embitter relations between the University and the community. In 1950, William Massey Birks (who had been elected governor of McGill in 1910) recalled the unhelpfulness of Principal Peterson's reputation during a public appeal for funds: 'Unfortunately one of the problems in raising the money was the Principal's unpopularity in the City. Perhaps the reason was that he never

Sir William Macdonald

really became a Canadian; an enthusiastic imperialist, he did not sufficiently realize Canada's place in that imperialism. All his summers were spent in England, where he educated his sons, and where for many years Lady Peterson remained.

'Montreal may have resented this implication of colonial inferiority. He did not easily "condescend to men of low estate". Moreover, with his fine classical mind went a subtlety which presented problems to his more forthright Canadian neighbours, to whom his course often seemed devious, and to which they tended to apply harsher terms.'

This unpopularity of the principal with the City extended at times to the students. At convocations the students' dislike might swell into an uncontrollable uproar.

One graduate, of the class of 1912, writes: 'The only time I saw much of Dr Peterson was at my graduation. This was held in the Royal Victoria College and was unbelievably noisy. Little could be heard. Peterson's deep drawling voice was well-known and easily imitated. When he addressed the students these imitations, as well as catcalls and the almost incessant ringing of cowbells, drowned practically everything. Such conduct was hard to understand, for Peterson had the reputation among the students of being a classical scholar. As such he was respected by those whom I knew'.

Principal Peterson could not take the grateful satisfaction of his predecessor that under his administration there had been no 'serious breaches of discipline, no college emeutes or rebellions'. His was not the fatherly presence of Principal Dawson, which had controlled the students with a firm but gentle dignity.

Though a number of students came to know his charm and his real concern for their welfare, many felt the coldness of his manner, and unduly resented it. Principal Peterson often sought to awe students with his 'salutary hauteur'. The effect was more embittering than salutary.

Despite all these tensions, Principal Peterson had a wide influence on the progress of McGill. His own students in classics, though never many, had the advantage of a teacher of rare learning. Moreover, the Faculty of Arts, though never keeping pace with the general growth of the university, did make gains. Several new chairs were endowed, including one of moral philosophy, and the

The Macdonald Physics Building

endowment of several existing chairs was increased. Scholarships were established.

Sir William was also able to bring about the opening of two new departments that were close to his heart – music and social science.

The Conservatorium of Music was to him almost an expansion of his work in classics. It was a similar ministry to the spirit, a release from the materialistic world. As he said at the opening of the McGill Conservatorium: 'Plato rightly said that music was given to men not with the sole view of pleasing their senses, but rather for appeasing the troubles of their souls . . . Long ago it was recognized as the panacea for the ills of human life; "when Orpheus played upon his lyre the heart of Pluto relented, Eurydice escaped, the wheel of Ixion stopped, the vultures ceased to torment Tityos, the thirst of Tantalus was forgotten, and the goddess of death did not remember to call away the infant or the aged from sweet life" '.

Principal Peterson also hoped to appease the troubles of men's souls through a department of social science. The suffering that accompanied industrialism had not weighed heavily on the thought of Victorian Montreal: such suffering had seemed less the problem of industrialism than an unchanging human need to be served by perpetual charity. Peterson, of a later generation, was more deeply aware of the great sea of human misery. The vision troubled him. Something more than charity was needed. Constructive effort awaited a social science to train and direct it.

In no city on earth, he believed, was a department of social science needed more than in Montreal. The city's efforts to relieve the wants of the poor were confused by racial and religious divisions. In a department of social science at the university the problem might be viewed with greater detachment, and the service might be rendered with greater unity. There was, perhaps, a certain shallowness in his understanding of the Montreal community, but, in any case, the department of social science at McGill was an expression of his honourable social consciousness.

Principal Peterson also had a Scottish interest in schools and a Scottish respect for their value. He took satisfaction in the new centre for the training of teachers at Macdonald College. He entered with helpfulness into Sir William Macdonald's plans, even though there was some difference of aim, as when Principal Peterson hoped to develop the teaching of music in the schools, while Sir

William Macdonald was more concerned with manual training. Principal Peterson was for a number of years chairman of the Protestant Committee of the Council of Public Instruction in Quebec, and seriously carried out his duties as a trustee.

But the scope of Principal Peterson's executive powers and the richness of his humanism did not find expression only in those aspects of the university's development that were relatively congenial to him. They were impressively seen in other ways.

Though not himself a scientist, he advanced McGill's scientific reputation immensely by the skill with which he recommended appointments. As a humanist, he was able to perceive in men their qualities of promise. He brought them to McGill, and at McGill they won in the new laboratories a world-wide fame.

Principal Peterson visited the Cavendish Laboratory at Cambridge (accompanied by Professor Cox of McGill) to interview Ernest Rutherford. 'Peterson and Cox came to the laboratory on Monday,' wrote Rutherford in a letter in July, 1894, 'and I saw Peterson twice for about an hour altogether.' Principal Peterson evidently made up his mind then and there. He wrote from England to Montreal, requesting the Board of Governors to sanction the appointment.

Working in the new laboratories at McGill, Rutherford, assisted by Frederick Soddy – another of Peterson's appointments – undertook research on the frontiers of physics. They proved the natural transmutation of elements and formed the theory of the radioactive disintegration of atoms. Though the full meaning of these researches was imperfectly seen at the time, these two young scientists at McGill were almost forming the nature of the Twentieth Century as the atomic age.

Rutherford and Soddy were Principal Peterson's two outstanding appointments. There were many others which showed how the Principal could perceive and welcome promise, even in fields of study not his own. Such, for example, was the appointment of Ernest William McBride to the new chair in zoology established at McGill by Lord Strathcona.

It was perhaps inevitable that McGill would lose these men, largely because of the very distinction they had won in her laboratories. Rutherford ultimately returned to Cambridge, to be professor of experimental physics and director of the Cavendish Laboratory.

Ernest Rutherford at McGill

Soddy was appointed professor of inorganic chemistry at Oxford. And McBride went to London to be professor of zoology at the Imperial College of Science, South Kensington.

What these men had done at McGill, and what McGill had enabled them to do, was enhanced by their later achievements elsewhere. The reputation of McGill in science, first established by the personal standing in the world of science of Sir William Dawson, had been greatly strengthened by the humanistic wisdom of his unscientific successor in his making of appointments.

In other developments at the university Principal Peterson proved his capacities in administration. He wished to raise McGill's importance and service beyond Montreal. He even launched a project to have McGill sponsor higher education in British Columbia. As early as 1899 he visited British Columbia to complete arrangements to affiliate the Vancouver and Victoria high schools with McGill, for courses in the first two years in Arts.

Among the undergraduates who studied classics under him at McGill was Lemuel Robertson. Peterson had selected Robertson in 1904 for a one year's lectureship in classics. Robertson was not only a promising scholar; he inspired the principal with the idea of using McGill's resources and prestige to establish a McGill College beyond the Rockies.

Principal Peterson took up the idea with vigour and competence. In 1906 the 'McGill University College of British Columbia' was established, with Dr Peterson as Principal. The quality of his leadership was seen not only in founding this faraway branch of McGill; it was seen no less in the wisdom with which he withdrew from the project when he considered that progress had been made to a point where withdrawal was preferable. In 1915, McGill, having made her contribution, merged her branch with the new University of British Columbia.

Principal Peterson saw in this experiment a value even greater than itself. 'The whole project,' he said, 'is the best possible illustration that Canada can have co-operation in higher education.'

Such leadership in education was seen in other ways. In 1911 Principal Peterson took the initiative in establishing the National Conference of Canadian Universities. He called the first meeting to McGill. He was elected the chairman of that meeting, and was then elected the Conference's first president. Twenty-two colleges and universities were the constituent members of the conference. The name was chosen with care to indicate that it was to be a body for consultation, not for control; it was to advise, not regulate. The first meetings discussed such questions as the standards of matriculation, the length of the academic terms and the conditions for the transfer of students. The growing importance of the Conference has proved its founder's foresight.

Not only nationally, but internationally, Principal Peterson played his role. He was appointed chairman of the Board of Trustees of the Carnegie Foundation for the Advancement of Teaching. He was an impressive representative of McGill at international gatherings, with his commanding manner, his skill with words. His academic honours were many.

Nor did his eminence in scholarship rest only on past achievements. He continued his study and research throughout his principalship. On one of his visits to England he made an important discovery in the library of Holkham Hall in Norfolk. There he came upon a manuscript of Cicero's speeches, dating from the ninth century and formerly belonging to Cluny. He used this manuscript for his edition of *Verrines*, published in 1907.

The last years of his principalship were preoccupied with the Great War. These war years gave him the satisfaction of a new singleness of purpose. He regarded his post as one of imperial influence and responsibility in a time of the Empire's testing. He would resist the emergence of a disturbing Canadian national feeling and would strive to make Canada's part in the war a contribution to imperialism.

Once again his extraordinary executive abilities were demonstrated. He organized McGill to serve the war, in every possible way, whether in scientific research or in military training. He had seen war approaching. With his active co-operation, McGill had become, in 1912, the first university in North America to establish an Officers' Training Corps.

He went to review McGill's units in their wartime service overseas, and was moved to hear the McGill yell echoing in foreign fields. 'The McGill yell is at all times an appealing cry,' he said, 'but to hear it on French soil gives one to think of the far-reaching influence of a wisely directed bequest to education. Truly, James McGill builded better than he knew.'

Macdonald College

For all his sincerity and devotion, rewarded with a wartime knighthood, his understanding of Canada's role was again mistaken. The constitutional result of the war was to be the Statute of Westminster, declaring that the Dominions are 'autonomous Communities within the British Empire, equal in status, in no way subordinate to one another in any aspect of their domestic or external affairs, though united by a common allegiance to the Crown, and freely associated as members of the British Commonwealth of Nations'.

Principal Peterson clearly foresaw such a development, and he struggled against it. He attacked the 'theorists' who spoke glibly of what they loved to call the 'golden link of the Crown'. His words were scathing: 'Their declared ideal for the future of the Empire is that of a group of "Associated Kingdoms" under the sovereignty of the Crown – so long as the Crown will undertake to remain overseas in England! This is the system by which they hope to remedy the "defects of the existing colonial status", which is said to "deter the growth of true Canadian patriotism and encourage a servile colonial loyalty that can never be consistent with self-respect!"'

'But is the golden link of the Crown likely to be binding enough for all coming time? It sometimes looks as though the advocates of this plan would not mind in the least if it should snap some day: then they would have the real independence which even now might seem to be their goal.'

Principal Peterson had come to Montreal feeling himself to be 'a stranger among strangers'. So to the end did he remain. And the end was near at hand.

On Sunday, January 12, 1919, though feeling ill, he had gone to lend his presence to a meeting in Emmanuel Church in Montreal where his countryman, Sir Harry Lauder, was to appear. It was a meeting to raise funds to benefit the widows and children of Scottish soldiers and sailors killed or disabled in the war. During the meeting he suffered a stroke, and fell from his chair to the floor.

There was to be no full recovery. His speech returned, but he never walked again. He submitted his resignation as principal of McGill and turned back to England. For some two years he survived, an invalid in a chair.

Sir William Peterson was a man with greatness. It was the tragedy of his life, and the loss to the university, that he proved unable quite to adjust the greatness that was within him to the new opportunities of time and place. In coming to McGill he had, as he said, 'torn himself up by the roots'. The roots had never really grown anew in a different, and uncongenial soil. Yet there is grace and dedication to his long years as McGill's principal. His leadership had an even deeper quality because, unlike that of his predecessor, it had to be given in ways often remote from his own tastes and desires. This mingling of a spectacular outward success, and an inescapable inward failure, has the drama of conflict.

In history, as in his lifetime, he remains a lonely figure amidst the greatness of his achievements. But the dignity of that loneliness, like the greatness of his achievements, will stand undiminished through 'all coming time'.

V

McGILL BETWEEN THE WARS

BY DAVID L. THOMPSON

A great war is more than the sum of multitudes of individual sufferings and bereavements: it is marked by the abandonment of beliefs that have proved insufficient, the formulation of new goals, the alteration of the climate of thought and feeling in which exist the institutions of our society: among which are the universities. It is my task to attempt to chart the course of McGill's history through two such crises: from the beginning of World War I to the end of World War II – this latter a date which many of our present students are too young to remember. I must keep my outlines simple and my pencil light; but first, for the record, a quotation from Fetherstonhaugh's *McGill University at War*: 'In 1914-18 the number of McGill men who enlisted in the Active Forces was 3,059; in 1939-45 the roll of men and women on active service totalled 5,568 . . . In the First Great War, 363 McGill men were killed in action or died on active service; in the Second Great War, the fatal casualties numbered 298 . . . '. These figures tell a story to which we may attend with sorrow and with pride; but that is not the story which is to be told here.

The First World War came, and the work of McGill was disrupted and depleted. The universities did not at that time enter into the thinking of the strategists: students, graduates, and staff played magnificent and often heroic parts, but they did so as individuals, or as groups of friends or associates, not as members of a *studium generale*. McGill was not asked (as it was to be asked in the Second War) to play an integral part in defence-research, and to provide courses of special training for military technicians. The whole

Sir Arthur Currie

climate was different. In the First War, an outstanding scientist, too old for the trenches but not too old to wear a uniform, spent four years trundling barrows around a railway station; students from even the upper years of the medical course were permitted and perhaps encouraged to enlist as rankers; there was no thought of a scheme to enable returning veterans to continue and complete their educations, often to levels which they could not have dreamed of attaining without the 'D.V.A.' subventions. Despite this and despite the appalling casualties, many did return, and university enrolment swelled: but the veteran of 1920, unlike his son of 1946, had little urgent sense of education as opportunity. Both, no doubt, found many aspects of student life pettifogging or even smug, after grim experiences in the forces; but where the son endured, the father protested. From the point of view of the teacher, the second crop of veteran students was a delight; they were mature, thoughtful, industrious, almost frighteningly earnest. The veterans of the first crop, in contrast, were often impatient, rowdy, uninterested; most of them (again the contrast!) would probably have come to the university had there been no war, and they resented the lost years, which to them opened no new doors. There were many exceptions, of course: and it is to be remembered that the proportion of young people choosing to come to college was much smaller then than it has since become, and that there were far fewer careers demanding a university degree.

Sir Auckland Geddes was appointed Principal, but withdrew without assuming office; he was succeeded by Sir Arthur Currie, who thereupon entered another phase of his astonishing career. There was nothing in his quite undistinguished early days as a school-teacher and then real-estate man in British Columbia to suggest that he would become the leader of the Canadian armies overseas, so successfully that Lloyd George and Smuts seriously thought of him as possibly supplanting Haig. There was little in his military career to suggest that he would make a great Principal of a great University (other institutions have been less fortunate with other generals). A score of anecdotes, some of them true, testify that he regarded the activities and the thought-patterns of his professors with incomprehension verging on incredulity. Yet he succeeded; and the academic world, usually jealous of an 'outsider' who has been granted power, regarded him with affection and respect. His decisions were prompt and fair; he could pass without effort from great dignity to jovial friendliness; he knew even very junior members of his staff, and kept himself informed about their personal problems. A wave of European scientists passed through Montreal in 1929; McGill entertained them, and I well remember how struck they were by Sir Arthur's impressive figure and voice: the military manner which he never lost would have seemed strange indeed in a French or German university.

Sir Arthur died in 1933, and there followed that disturbing period in which it was unkindly said that McGill had established a new two-year course, leading to the degree of ex-Principal. We had A. E. Morgan, then Lewis Douglas, two very dissimilar personalities; and there were long interregna, not shortened by the doubts which the then Chancellor (Sir Edward Beatty) seemed to entertain about the necessity of having a Vice-Chancellor at all. Under these conditions it was difficult for the University, as a whole, to make steady forward progress. When Dr James took office on January 1st, 1940, it was at a time when it was exceptionally difficult to foresee the shape or outcome of the War that filled our minds; few of us had any conviction about the future, except that it would bring change; and none, I dare say, was optimistic enough to expect that this young and obviously dynamic man would remain, to serve and guide the University, through an era that has already lasted twenty years.

It must be remembered, too, that the thirties were marked not only by changing leaderships, but also by the Depression. The effect upon the University was indirect, rather than direct; salaries were cut, but then prices fell; and on the whole the teaching staff suffered less and had more security than those in other professions; enrolment kept up, because there were no jobs to tempt young people not to come to college. On the other hand, it was next to impossible, both economically and psychologically, to take bold forward steps in such troubled days. There were developments here and there, of course; but on the whole it would not be unfair to say that, for one reason or another, McGill marked time during the thirties. One thing that could be done, and was done, during that period, holds little interest for the outside world: the Statutes were thoroughly revised (twice), and all administrative processes, both academic and non-academic, were surveyed and made more mod-

Lewis W. Douglas

ern and efficient; no major change in this direction has been necessary since.

One well-defined group must be exempted from the criticism implied in my second paragraph: those who returned from the war to become members of the staff of the Faculty of Engineering. They formed a close-knit and dedicated coterie; they inherited a building which had been thoroughly rehabilitated after the fire of 1907, and a new and more practical curriculum which had been worked out immediately before the war, and to which they gave' full allegiance. There was a long series of Deans (MacKay, Brown, O'Neill, Jamieson) who, though of course not all of the same age, were of the same generation and shared similar experience and similar habits of thought; so, too, did many of their professorial colleagues. Under these circumstances, it is not surprising that the School soon acquired a reputation for the excellence of its training towards the Bachelor's degree; training beyond this was not then in demand. Most of these men were well known in the outside world as consultants and were associated with enterprises of great national 'pith and moment'. This enhanced their standing with the students, geared their teaching to the most up-to-date practice, and provided them with invaluable 'contacts'; that it was also very remunerative was regarded as a rather sordid coincidence.

In fact, however, this pattern was not in harmony with a tide of change that began slowly seeping through the other major Faculties. As I look back over the years, including the decade before I came to McGill in 1928; it seems to me that the greatest change has been the increasing emphasis placed upon research and the training of graduate students. Today this is the criterion by which a university is judged by its peers, but it was not always so: Mendel, Darwin, Pasteur, Marie Curie, Freud, even Einstein, did not hold university positions during their greatest investigating years. It may seem strange to say this, since the most famous research ever carried out at McGill dates back to the beginning of the century; but this was the exception that proves the rule, and in fact McGill did not do very much homage (at the time!) to Rutherford, and did very little indeed – a demonstratorship, which was not renewed – for Soddy.

McGill was neither the first nor the last great university to accept productive research as one of its principal responsibilities to the

Sir Edward Beatty

community; the formation of the National Research Council of Canada in 1917 was a straw that showed which way the wind was blowing – and for many years (though not now!) little more than a straw, as far as direct aid to research in the universities was concerned. In our own campus, the establishment of the Faculty of Graduate Studies and Research, in 1923, was a milestone: true enough, Master's degrees and even occasional Doctorates had been granted from the beginning of the century, but always by the undergraduate or professional faculties or committees thereof, and (as far as one can see from the scanty records) in a somewhat haphazard manner. The first tasks of the new Faculty were to regularize these procedures and, especially, to draw up firmer rules and regulations for the degree, then still regarded in some quarters as new-fangled and Germanic, of Doctor of Philosophy. These revised regulations have changed but little through the years, save that more and more Departments have come under this umbrella; and it is interesting to note that even when the degree was thus firmly established, McGill was in no hurry to confer it. Several years separated the second from the first; today there are approximately a hundred per annum. In some subjects, such as Chemistry and Physics, a pattern soon became set. Toronto was, for very many years, the only other English-Canadian university to offer the Ph.D. and drew most of its candidates from Ontario; even now, despite the post-war growth and energy of many other graduate schools, in the natural sciences the McGill Ph.D. is still a powerful lodestone to the Maritimes and to the West.

It takes more than rules and regulations to build a graduate school: money and men are required. In the twenties, in the natural sciences, we had but two men who held the accolade of the Royal Society of London: appropriately enough, for the beginning of a new era, their names were Adams and Eve. The need for a new slant, a new emphasis, was perhaps first perceived by the Dean of Medicine, C. F. Martin: subtle, farsighted, and persuasive, he understood that he must bring in distinguished investigators and give them adequate support. He brought in Penfield and Cone and fostered the growth of the Montreal Neurological Institute around them: he brought Collip in Biochemistry, Babkin in Physiology, and Murray and Smith in Bacteriology; he got generous Rockefeller help, not only for the M.N.I., but also for the University Clinic in the Royal Victoria Hospital, where, under the 'mild and magnificent eye' of Meakins there grew up (to name some of our own present professors only) Browne, Christie and Venning. A later, brilliantly successful but tragically short-lived appointment, was that of Lyman Duff in Pathology, which introduced the experimental approach into this most central of all the medical sciences.

In the natural sciences the pattern was different and developed more slowly; I have spoken of the years during which McGill perforce marked time, and for a variety of reasons it happened that very few appointments were made at senior levels by importing scholars from elsewhere. What did happen was that a few men, such as Maass in Chemistry and Foster in Physics, who had long been devoted investigators and won international recognition, began to rise in the hierarchy and eventually became Chairmen of their Departments; and their enthusiasm and example infected others. On the Arts side the progress was slower still: at one time there was not a single member of the teaching staff in Section II of the Royal Society of Canada; here the 'breakthrough' took place towards the end of my period, when several senior vacancies in Economics and Political Science were filled by young and active men, vigorous in research. In Engineering, as I have implied, consultative work was rated far ahead of any laboratory work that could be undertaken on the campus. But even where progress was slow, it was steady; and there is today no sector of the University that does not have its active research programmes.

It was not till after the Second War that these developments took the now popular form of 'Institutes', devoted almost wholly to research and seldom entered by an undergraduate: the only early examples were the Institute of Parasitology at Macdonald College, and a small group of laboratories for Industrial and Cellulose Chemistry. But the change in atmosphere preceded the translation into physical form; it came to be recognized that there were members of the staff who could serve the University best by giving nearly all their time to research and their graduate students, and little or none to students in other Faculties. More important, creative productivity was given more and more weight in selecting candidates for appointment or promotion.

This evolution, necessary for any university that aspired to first-class standing, did not fail to create difficulties. The training

Wilder Penfield, O.M.

of graduate students takes a great deal of time, and expansion of staff would have been necessary even if the other faculties had remained constant in enrolment. In laboratory subjects, graduate students also take up a great deal of space, and the older buildings, not designed with any such evolution in mind, became uncomfortably crowded – and remain so. Even where the direct costs of research (purchase of equipment and supplies, employment of research assistants and the like) are fully covered by grants from external bodies, its indirect costs (professors' salaries, provision and servicing of space, maintenance of library facilities, and so on) have to be met by the University, and it is probably fortunate that the task of realistically assessing the total is so formidably difficult that nobody attempts it. It is, indeed, difficult enough for the University to keep accounts for all the scores of special research funds which it must administer!

It is almost certainly wrong and unfair to single out for special mention a few of the burgeoning research activities of the thirties, yet how can one fail to recall the work of Maass on the 'critical state', of Steacie in photo-chemistry, of Hibbert on cellulose and lignin; Foster's transition from spectrometry to nuclear physics; the unravelling of the anterior pituitary hormones by Collip; Babkin's studies of the digestive glands; Penfield on Jacksonian epilepsy; and – but I really dare not go further!

Yet if I am to name names at all, I must certainly recall a few of those who were renowned chiefly as teachers and are affectionately remembered as such by thousands of graduates. Such a list must, of course, be headed by the name of Stephen Leacock, a name known to more people, all around the world, than any other associated with McGill (perhaps all others put together, even including Osler and Rutherford?). Yet, if he had never written a line, or never gone on a lecture tour, and had thus remained unknown elsewhere, he would have made an indelible mark upon his students; he was outstandingly one of 'those regal Dons, with hearts of gold and lungs of bronze' and his bubbling wit and his own huge enjoyment of it are unforgettable.

Witty, too, in a quieter vein, was Woodhead, who always struck one as a reincarnation of Charles Lamb; and both were 'Blue-coat boys'. Hatcher could etch the outlines of organic chemistry into his students' minds with the acid of a touch of sarcasm, yet take

The Neurological Institute

endless pains to help those who seemed to need and deserve advice.
Keys presented the elements of Physics to generations of students
with lucid kindliness and infinite patience; Gillson, cadaverous and
sardonic, despised the kind of mathematics that undergraduates
require ('arithmetic', he called it), but taught it brilliantly; and,
from the early thirties almost to the present day, one was always
conscious of the presence in the background of T. H. Matthews,
the Registrar, unweariedly prompting and advising, smoothing
pathways and untying red tape. Every graduate will recall many
more who served the University well: *vixere fortes ante Agamemnona.*

The growing size and complexity of the University entailed an
increase in the purely administrative staff, and an increase in the
administrative duties devolving upon the teaching staff. In the mid-
thirties, a chance enquiry from a foreign government prompted the
formation of a University Scholarships Committee, which (like the
Time-table Committee and several others) has ever since demanded selfless and constant service from its changing membership. The
days when a Department might be divided into those who lectured
on Monday, Wednesday, and Friday, and those who lectured on
the other days, 'and never the twain shall meet', have long since
gone: most of us now are slaves to the telephone and the dictaphone.
It is natural to think nostalgically of a more spacious, less bustling
past: and yet – surely the idea of a university is more nearly fulfilled
when scholars of many disciplines are constantly brought together,
even in the desiccated atmosphere of a committee meeting? A word
should also be said of the welding function of our Faculty Club,
the envy of all our visitors: the atmosphere here is noticeably less
desiccated.

I hope I have not yielded too much to my own special interests
in focusing attention on the development of the research-function
of the University as the outstanding theme of these decades. Other
themes could, perhaps, have been emphasized with equal justifica-
tion. The Burnside Estate, as James McGill bequeathed it to us,
was far outside the city; long before the First War, the city had
grown up to and around it, squeezing the University, as it were,
against the mountain behind. This intimate contact, at first purely
geographical, began more recently to acquire sociological meaning, as contacts between the University and the city became wider
and richer. There were the practising lawyers and doctors who

Stephen Leacock

gave up some of their scanty time to teaching; there were the professors who were called into consultation by Montreal's great industries. The establishment of new courses and new degrees increasingly reflected the felt needs of the community. Members of the McGill staff went out, to speak to service clubs and the like; members of the public came in, to attend concerts organized by the Faculty of Music, the various 'shows' put on by the students, and especially the now-numerous evening Extension courses, which bring on to the campus as many persons as do the regular programmes of the degree-granting faculties. There are still misunderstandings to be smoothed out, and probably there always will be; but surely McGill stands firmly in the heart of Montreal, and the cleavage between Town and Gown is gone forever.

Visit of H.R.H. Princess Elizabeth to McGill, Oct. 30, 1951

VI

THE LINK WITH THE FUTURE
1945 - 1959
BY F. CYRIL JAMES

CANADA's attitude to its universities has changed several times. Before the middle of the nineteenth century (the panic of 1857 may mark the turning point) few people in Canada had any interest in higher education. Priests were needed so that the Seminary which Bishop Laval had founded in Quebec was important, but doctors, lawyers and other professional men could be imported (when needed) from England or Scotland. James McGill was far ahead of his generation in thinking that Canada should educate its own sons.

From 1857 to the end of the first World War, the ripples of a new tide became increasingly apparent. Individuals began to realize that they could get ahead more rapidly if they set out with a university diploma in their suitcase, so that student enrolment grew steadily. Engineers, lawyers, physicians, accountants, school teachers – all of these began to play a more important role in the life of Canada, and each of them had to start his career at a Canadian university unless he was wealthy enough to study overseas. Those who could afford it still preferred to go to universities in England, France or the United States.

This tide of individual desire for a university degree continued in full flood after 1918, and is running stronger than ever today, but new and complex forces beat upon Canadian universities during the years between the wars. Research became a magic word – research in medicine to prolong human life, research in chemistry to enlarge the profits of the pulp and paper industry, research in business cycles to explain the depression and make it palatable to

113

F. Cyril James

its victims. In Canada, the universities were the centres for this research, particularly McGill and Toronto, so that the quiet persistence of searchers for truth mingled with the desire of the undergraduates for professional success on each Canadian campus.

Research proved its importance during the second World War, and Canada's part of that story has been splendidly told by Eggleston and Fetherstonhaugh.[1] The problems of the war years also brought into focus the importance of trained men and women to Canada as a nation – both in the armed services and in the economic development of the country – at the very moment when Canada was, for the first time in its long history, proudly evolving a consciousness of its own nationality independent of both Great Britain and the United States, although related to both in friendly partnership.

Universities were of vital importance to the defence, the welfare and the prosperity of Canada. The novelty of this idea has worn off in two decades of oratorical reiteration, but the concept was revolutionary during the early years of the war. During the long critical months of 1940 and 1941, a government committee under the chairmanship of General H. F. McDonald wrestled with the problems of demobilzation and rehabilitation that would arise when the war was over. Its conclusions were startling. Every veteran who was academically qualified, and eager to attend university, should be encouraged to do so at the expense of the Government of Canada. Each university should receive supplementary financial aid from the Government of Canada to enable it to provide better educational opportunities for the returning veterans. This new concept was adopted by the Government and officially announced, in October 1941, under the innocuous cloak of Order-in-Council P.C.7633. A similar programme was to be adopted shortly afterwards by both Great Britain and the United States. Canada was blazing a trail, and proclaiming that the universities were an essential part of its new national identity.

Today, when the new tide is in full flood, it is easy to appraise its significance. It was less easy on Monday, January 8, 1945, when 233 demobilized veterans, most of them still in Air Force uniforms, walked across the snow-covered campus of McGill University to

[1] Wilfred Eggleston: *Scientists at War*, Toronto 1950; R. C. Fetherstonhaugh: *McGill University at War*, Montreal 1947.

Purvis Hall

the Macdonald Physics Building for the first lecture of their university course. Nothing like this had ever happened at any university in Canada. The Principal, Dean Cyrus Macmillan, Professor David A. Keys and the President of the Students' Society (Mr John Costigan) each reflected in their brief speeches of welcome a sense that this occasion was the beginning of something new.

The dominant theme of those speeches was, however, appreciation of what the veterans had done for Canada and of our desire to help them. Two years earlier, the Senate of McGill University had resolved that, except in the Faculty of Medicine where limitation of laboratory and clinical facilities made such a policy impossible, no qualified student who came to us from the armed services of Canada, Great Britain or the United States would be refused admission. Under the leadership of W. H. Hatcher and F. F. Osborne, the University Time Table Committee had worked out plans to use every classroom and laboratory as many hours a day as was humanly possible. To meet the needs of veterans who might be demobilized during the winter or spring, and to permit full utilization of buildings throughout the calendar year, it was decided that students from the armed forces would be admitted in January and in May (as well as at the traditional date in September) and a committee under the chairmanship of Professor David A. Keys was appointed to administer the programme of parallel and overlapping courses that resulted.

The Board of Governors had played its part in this planning. Although new buildings could not be constructed during the war years unless – as in the case of the annex to the Montreal Neurological Institute and the additional laboratories in the attics of the Physics Building – they were needed for government purposes, the Board had acquired Purvis Hall to house the School of Commerce and Beatty Hall for the Graduate Nurses, as well as several other houses on University Street and Pine Avenue. Mr J. W. McConnell, in 1943, led a campaign which added more than $7,000,000 to the general endowments for the purpose of raising the salaries of the teaching staff; and this made possible the recruiting of a small number of juniors as well as the retention of many senior members of the staff who would otherwise have retired.

All of these plans went smoothly into effect on January 8, 1945, and the whole University began that superb effort (destined to last for more than five years) on which it had voluntarily resolved. No chapter in McGill's history is finer than the story of that effort: the record scintillates with un-numbered personal incidents and individual memories.

The first six months of the programme were the easiest. During the summer of 1945, hostilities came to an end and the number of veteran students seeking admission to Canadian universities suddenly rose to levels that had not been contemplated in our wartime planning. At McGill, on VE day, the total student enrolment (including the veterans who had already started their courses) was 3,933. A year later, in the autumn of 1946, this figure had risen to 6,366 and during the 1948-49 session it reached a peak of 8,240.

Unless McGill could somehow find additional space for lecture rooms, laboratories and student residences, the whole programme would break down! The construction of new buildings would take too long, even if the necessary permits could be obtained, so that an intensive search for appropriate accommodation began after VJ Day and, on Wednesday, September 26, 1945, McGill took over from the Royal Canadian Air Force the land and buildings of Number 9 Air Observer School at St Jean, Quebec. Through the cooperation of the Honourable Douglas Abbott (at that time Minister of Defence) the University was able to obtain from military stores beds, blankets, tables, and other things necessary to furnish the empty huts, and by Friday night 700 students had come into residence. On the morning of Monday, October 1st, regular classes began.

In the official records of the University this establishment at St Jean (enlarged in 1946 when McGill took over from the R.C.A.F. the adjoining buildings of Number 9 Repair Depot) was known as Dawson College. The name was appropriate when we recall Sir William Dawson's early difficulties in regard to buildings, but the students more often referred to the College as Dawson City or, less affectionately, Lower Slobbovia. The names were apt during the winter months, and even more so when the spring thaw resulted in a sea of glutinous mud!

Air Force huts, admirable for their intended purpose, are not ideal college buildings, and the experiment of Dawson College succeeded (as thousands of its ex-students still testify with fierce loyalty) only because of the personal efforts of a small band of men.

P. W. MacFarlane, the Superintendent of Buildings and Grounds
who had served as a sergeant-major of the Black Watch in the first
World War, worked like a Trojan to get the buildings into the best
possible shape and created laboratories and library facilities as well
as residence accommodation. A. H. S. Gillson, who had command-
ed the R.C.A.F. Navigation School during the war, returned to his
post as Professor of Mathematics and was promptly appointed the
first Vice-Principal of Dawson College, with Carleton Craig as his
assistant. These men, together with W. H. Hatcher (who succeeded
Gillson as Vice-Principal of Dawson College when the latter became President of the University of Manitoba), Clifford Knowles
(the newly-appointed university chaplain) and E. M. Orlick (in
charge of Athletics) created a living and lively academic community, and they were aided in their task by many other members of
the teaching staff who commuted week by week to conduct their
classes. When Dawson College closed its doors in the spring of 1950,
and the buildings were handed back to the Government, the memory of those five years had become firmly embedded in the traditions of McGill.

Meanwhile on Founder's Day, October 6, 1946, the members of

The War Memorial Hall

the University had attended a solemn memorial service for the Mc-Gill men and women who gave their lives during both world wars. Colonel the Reverend G. G. D. Kilpatrick, chaplain of the Black Watch in France a generation earlier, and Major the Reverend Clifford Knowles, who had come from his recent military service to become the first Chaplain of McGill University, conducted that service. Field Marshal the Viscount Alexander of Tunis laid the foundation stone of the War Memorial Hall and Swimming Pool, to build which graduates from all corners of the world had sub-scribed. This was the enduring expression to future generations of our debt to those who gave the last full measure of devotion, but during all the days of those years from 1945 to 1950 the deep debt of the older men to the young veterans was so continuously expressed in a thousand ways of friendship and help that none who lived through that period will forget the experience.

By the summer of 1951, most of the veterans had graduated: those who remained at the University were enrolled in Dentistry, Law, Medicine or the Faculty of Graduate Studies. During the 1953-54 session student enrolment fell to 6,550 – a high figure com-pared to the years before 1939 but the lowest since the end of the war.

New forces were, however, creating new problems for all Canad-ian universities. The birth rate in Canada, which had declined during the depressed 'thirties, rose sharply during the war years and statis-ticians pointed out that larger numbers of young people – already alive and in school – would be knocking on the doors of Canadian universities from 1960 onwards. The growing recognition of the importance of university education also suggested that a larger proportion of Canada's youth would seek admission. A growing proportion of a larger population! Experts began to predict that the number of university students in 1965 would be twice as large as it had been in the early 'fifties, and that by 1970 it would have tripled.

Deepening realization of the fact that universities were import-ant to the development of Canada as a nation underlined the fact that this problem transcended provincial boundaries. The financial assistance from Ottawa, paid as a supplementary grant for the education of veterans, would come to an end when the last veteran had graduated, and the National Conference of Canadian Univer-

The Redpath Library

sities, in 1948, petitioned the Government of Canada for a new peace-time programme of financial support.

The Government responded in April, 1949, by creating a Royal Commission under the chairmanship of the Right Honourable Vincent Massey to survey the whole problem of national development in the arts, letters and sciences. Extended hearings were held by the Commission in all parts of the country, and among the submissions there were many from individual universities or from university groups, so that when the final Report appeared in the early summer of 1951 (at the moment when the National Conference of Canadian Universities was holding its annual meetings at McGill) there was widespread satisfaction in the Royal Commission's statement that:

> ' The Universities are provincial institutions; but they are much more than that . . . They serve the national cause in so many ways, direct and indirect, that theirs must be regarded as the finest of contributions to national strength and unity.' [2]

Within a few weeks of the publication of the Report the Prime Minister of Canada, the Right Honourable Louis St. Laurent, asked the House of Commons for an appropriation of $7,100,000 to provide financial grants toward the operating expenditures of all Canadian universities during the 1951-52 academic session. The leaders of the Opposition spoke in favour of the proposal and, on June 19, 1951, the House adopted it without dissent. The national importance to Canada of the work of her universities, dimly perceived during the dark days of the second World War, was now officially recognized, and although constitutional controversies [3] made it impossible for McGill and other universities in Quebec to accept these grants during the nineteen-fifties, there can be no question that the Report of the Massey Commission marks the opening of a new era in Canadian higher education.

McGill played its part in these exciting developments on the national scheme, even though it derived little financial advantage from them, but important developments were at the same time under way on our own campus. To meet the long-range needs of the University, formulated by the McGill Development Com-

(2) *Report of the Royal Commission on National Development in the Arts, Letters and Sciences*, Ottawa, 1951, p.132.

(3) Cf. *Report of the Royal Commission of Inquiry on Constitutional Problems*, Quebec, 1957, especially Volume II.

mittee, it was announced in the Annual Report for 1948-49 that additional capital funds, aggregating $26,750,000 would be needed before 1960 for the endowment of new professorships and the construction of new buildings. In the autumn of 1948 the first instalment of $8,000,388 was raised during the course of a financial campaign under the chairmanship of Mr G. Blair Gordon, and six years later, during the autumn of 1956, a second campaign, led by Mr R. E. Powell and Mr J. A. Fuller, produced a further $9,172,730.

These campaigns, successful as they were, do not tell the whole story since many substantial gifts, some of the largest of them anonymous, were received from friends of the University at other times. To present in this chapter the detailed record that has been published each year in the Annual Report would be inappropriate, so that the following summary table must serve to indicate the growth of the University; but mention must be made of Mr J. W. McConnell and Mr Walter M. Stewart, the outstanding benefactors of McGill during the past twenty years. Each of them served on the Board of Governors for a quarter of a century; each has been continually interested in all that concerns the life of McGill. Because of their desire for anonymity on many occasions, few people know the extent to which they have nurtured the University that they have loved with deep affection, but the record of their help is inextricably woven into the tapestry of our history.

The Growth of McGill

	1919-20	1938-39	1958-59
Operating Revenues	$1,182,334	$2,334,466	$14,595,982
Invested Endowments	12,648,988	16,851,751	61,093,155
Lands, Buildings & Equipment	8,521,168	13,727,739	30,227,714
Student Enrolment	2,390	3,286	7,717

The above figures reflect the developments of the last twenty years, with the situation on the morrow of the first World War for comparison. Two other statistics can be added for clarification. From 1939 to 1959 the total area of the buildings used for education and research increased from 1,186,586 square feet to 2,931,845 square feet. During the same period the number of members of the

Tyndale Hall

teaching staff rose from 545 to 1,128, so that in both cases the increase has been proportionately greater than the increase in student enrolment.

These statistics are no more than the dry bones of university history. To infuse life into the record, we must recall the surging activity that the statistics crystallize momentarily into a formal pattern. To describe this activity in detail would require a history of each department, and the stories of hundreds of individual teachers. It must suffice to mention a few of the innovations.

As early as 1944, the University started the construction of a cyclotron to carry further the work that Rutherford had started, in the Macdonald Physics Building in 1908; and in the same year George H. T. Kimble was brought out from England, with the consent of the Admiralty which released him from his naval duties in order that he might set up a Department of Geography at McGill. Kenneth Hare followed as soon as the Royal Air Force could release him, and the Department has steadily expanded its programme of teaching and research until today its activities extend from the McGill Sub-Arctic Laboratories on Knob Lake (and sometimes a station on Ellesmere Island) to the tropic area served by the Bellairs Research Institute, a McGill outpost in Barbados. McGill biologists also make use of these outposts, as well as of the Morgan Woods at Senneville, given to the University by Mr J. W. McConnell and the Morgan family in 1941, and of Mont St Hilaire, which was bequeathed to McGill in 1958 by Brigadier Hamilton Gault.

In that same year, 1944, the University and the Royal Victoria Hospital collaborated in the creation of the Allan Memorial Institute of Psychiatry, the first of its kind in Canada, and D. Ewen Cameron started to bring together the team of outstanding colleagues which has developed the Institute to the point where it today has a world-wide reputation. A Department of Anaesthesia was created soon after, which, under the leadership of Wesley Bourne, Harold R. Griffith and, today, James G. Robson, has carried out a programme of research that can only be appreciated by those whose pain has thereby been relieved.

In 1948, largely as a result of the persistent enthusiasm of Mr W. M. Birks, who was then the senior governor of the University, an oecumenical Faculty of Divinity (the first of its kind in Canada) was set up to train ministers for the Anglican and the United

Churches – both of which agreed to collaborate in the experiment for an initial period of five years. Dr. James S. Thomson was persuaded to leave the Presidency of the University of Saskatchewan to become Dean of the new Faculty and, at the end of five years, the experiment was such an outstanding success that the University and the Churches spontaneously insisted on its permanence.

Among the uncovenanted benefits that McGill received from the Faculty of Divinity was the creation, in 1952, of the Institute of Islamic Studies, centring around Professor Wilfred Cantwell Smith, and endowed by the Rockefeller Foundation. Muslim scholars from all parts of the world have come to McGill, and western scholars are trying to interpret to Christendom the problems of the Islamic world in our generation – problems that confront us in newspaper headlines from areas as widely separate as Indonesia, Pakistan and Egypt, problems that have profound significance for the peace of the world and the welfare of mankind.

Another, completely different, window on the world was opened in the same year by the creation of the Institute of International Air Law, but it is the characteristic of a university that new things and old are always blending. The training of teachers for the Protestant schools of Quebec, for which McGill has been responsible ever since Sir William Dawson founded the McGill Normal School more than a century ago, was reorganized in 1952 under the aegis of a newly created Institute of Education which integrated the studies carried on within both McGill College and Macdonald College, so that they formed the basic pattern for the new degree of Bachelor of Education.

These are no more than samples of the changing pattern of life at McGill since the end of the second World War. Many others could be mentioned. But change involves loss as well as gain, and memory recalls with pride and with affection the men who no longer march beside us. On the Board of Governors, only Senator A. K. Hugesson remains from the twenty-five men who sat around the oval table in the Council Room at the outbreak of war in 1939; although Mr J. W. McConnell and Mr Walter M. Stewart are still actively interested in McGill as Governors Emeritus. Of those who are members of the Senate today only one, Professor William Rowles, was a member twenty years ago.

The roster of those who served McGill, many with their lives,

The Cyclotron Magnets

during these difficult years, is for the University an imperishable page in its history: for us who remain, a garland of friendship remembered with personal sadness. Sir Edward Beatty, who had served McGill as its Chancellor since 1920, with strong personal devotion, died in 1943, His successor, Morris Wilson, died three years later as a result of the strain that heavy war time responsibilities had placed upon his willing shoulders. Chief Justice Orville Tyndale, the first graduate of McGill to become its Chancellor, died in 1952. To each of these men, as well as to Mr B. C. Gardner, who served as Chancellor from 1952-1957 and to Mr R. E. Powell, who now holds that office, McGill stands in debt and, if a personal note may be permitted, I should like to express my own sense of obligation. Men of widely differing personality and aptitude, each made his individual contribution.

Among the many others whom death has taken from us, memory recalls the strong personalities of W. M. Birks, Walter W. Chipman, Walter Molson and Arthur Purvis, who served McGill as members of the Board of Governors. Ernie Brown, a Dean beloved of Engineers; Jimmy Simpson, Fred Smith and Lyman Duff – each recalled by generations of medical students as the Dean of their years at McGill; Cyrus Macmillan, and Albert Gillson, well-remembered Deans of the Faculty of Arts and Science; Prescott Mowry of Dentistry. None of these will be forgotten by those who worked with them, and knew their friendship. P. W. MacFarlane, Superintendent of Buildings and Grounds for more than twenty years; Anne Liston, the senior telephone operator, and Bill Gentleman, remembered by thousands of students – the list could be prolonged. Each of us finds memory calling-up another, and still another, familiar friend. So many changes have occurred during the past two decades as a result of retirement and resignation, as well as by death, that six Deans have followed one another in the Faculty of Medicine; four in the Faculty of Arts and Science, the Faculty of Engineering and the Faculty of Law; three in the Faculty of Dentistry and two in Agriculture, Divinity and Graduate Studies.

Change, like the sparkling kaleidoscope of sunlight on rippling waters, is the immediate impression created by McGill's record during this period. But the changing kaleidoscope is superficial: it is the pattern of light that changes with each ripple, not the deep water.

THE LINK WITH THE FUTURE

McGill University is still the product of all her yesterdays. The Founder's Elm still flourishes on the rural farm which has today become the geographical centre of a great city. The portico of the Arts Building, surmounted by the familiar cupola, has been a land-mark to Montrealers for more than a century. Tradition is even more durable than stone and copper, and the continuity of men's devotion to a university is greater than we realize. T. W. M. Cameron, J. S. Foster, J. U. MacEwan, Wilder Penfield, Frank Scott and David L. Thomson were Professors at McGill in 1939: they are still members of the McGill family and the years have added not only to their laurels but to the affection with which they are regarded by colleagues and students alike. Eighteen others who now hold the rank of Professor have been members of the teaching staff for twenty years or more, as have more than eighty who hold the rank of Associate Professor. The number of those members of the University who are graduates of McGill, and who imbibed its traditions during their students years, is many times larger.

No man can write the concluding paragraph to the story of a university that is still alive. The motto of James McGill *In domino confido* is as appropriate to his vision as the motto of the University *Grandescunt aucta labore* is to the herculean labours of Dawson. Both are a part of McGill's heritage, and they are enough. Faith and works are blended in the effort to adapt to the solution of today's problems the heritage of all our yesterdays.

> The years which the locust that eateth
> all our years hath eaten, perchance these
> pages may restore them to you.

INDEX

INDEX

INDEX

Royal Victoria Hospital, 23, 106, 125

Rutherford, Ernest Rutherford 1st Baron, 19, 91, 103, 108, 125

Ruttan, Robert Fulford, 19

St. Hilaire, 125

St. Jean, 118

St. Laurent, Rt. Hon. Louis, 122

Ste. Anne-de-Bellevue, 16, 82, 86

Scott, F. R., 129

Senneville, 125

Seven Years' War, 27, 30

Sherbrooke, Street, 23, 81

Simpson, James, 128

Smith, Frederick, 105, 128

Smith, Wilfred Cantwell, 126

Smuts, Jan, 100

Soddy, Frederick, 19, 91, 93, 103

Staff Development Institutes, 16

Stanley St. Presbyterian Church, 67

Stcacic, E. W. R., 108

Stewart, Walter, M., 123, 126

Strachan, Bishop John, 40, 41

Strathcona & Mount Royal, 1st Baron, 16, 75, 79, 86, 91

Strathcona, Lady, 19

Stuart, Prince Charles Edward, 39

Students' Society, 117

Sub-Arctic Laboratories, 125

Sun, 47

Teachers, School for, 82

Thompson, David, 32

Thomson, David, L. 129

Thomson, Rev. Dr. J. S., 126

Todd, Isaac, 33

Trinity College (Dublin), 46

Trollope, Anthony, 43

Tyndale, Orville, 128

United College, 16

University College of Dundee, 75, 77

University of British Columbia, 93

University of Manitoba, 119

University of Toronto, 105

Vancouver, 93

V.E. Day, 118

Venning, E. H., 106

Victoria, City of, 93

V.J. Day, 118

War Memorial Hall & Swimming Pool, 120

Waterloo, 40

Westminster, Statute of, 96

Wilson, Morris, 128

Wolfe, Maj. Gen. James, 21, 30, 39

Woodhead, W. D., 108

Workman Building for Mechanical Engineering, 63

World War I, 94, 98, 100, 113

World War II, 98, 106, 115, 122

World War II Veterans, 115, 117, 118, 119, 120